TALES OF MEDIEVAL DUBLIN

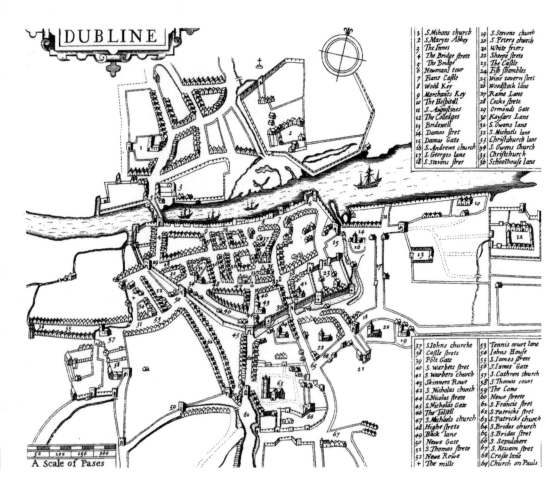

Dublin, 1610, from John Speed's *Theatre of the empire of Great Britaine* (1611/12).

Tales of Medieval Dublin

Sparky Booker & Cherie N. Peters

EDITORS

FOUR COURTS PRESS

This book was set in 11.5 on 16 point Adobe Garamond by
Mark Heslington, Scarborough, North Yorkshire for
FOUR COURTS PRESS
7 Malpas Street, Dublin 8, Ireland
www.fourcourtspress.ie
and in North America for
FOUR COURTS PRESS
c/o ISBS, 920 N.E. 58th Avenue, Suite 300, Portland, OR 97213.

A catalogue record for this title
is available from the British Library.

ISBN 978–1-84682–497–5 | Paperback
ISBN 978–1-84682–496–8 | Hardback

SPECIAL ACKNOWLEDGMENT
The publication of this book was suppported by
Dublin City Council

Comhairle Cathrach
Bhaile Átha Cliath
Dublin City Council

Printed in England
by CPI Antony Rowe, Chippenham, Wiltshire

Contents

❧

Contents

List of illustrations

FIGURES

PLATES   (between p. 148 and p. 149)

Abbreviations

AFM   *Annála ríoghachta Éireann: Annals of the kingdom of Ireland by the Four Masters, from the earliest period to the year 1616*, ed. and trans. J. O'Donovan, 7 vols (Dublin, 1851)

AI   *The Annals of Inisfallen (MS Rawlinson B503)*, ed. and trans. S. Mac Airt (Dublin, 1951)

Alen's Reg. *Calendar of Archbishop Alen's register, c.1172–1534*, ed. C. MacNeill (Dublin, 1950)

AT   *The Annals of Tigernach*, ed. and trans. W. Stokes, 2 vols (Felinfach, 1993)

AU   *Annála Uladh, Annals of Ulster from the earliest times to the year 1541*, ed. and trans. W.M. Hennessy and B. MacCarthy, 4 vols (2nd ed. Dublin, 1998); *The Annals of Ulster (to AD 1131)*, ed. and trans. S. Mac Airt and G. Mac Niocaill (Dublin, 1983)

BL   British Library, London

BL Add. MS British Library Additional manuscript

CARD   *Calendar of ancient records of Dublin in the possession of the municipal corporation*, ed. J.T. Gilbert and R.M. Gilbert, 19 vols (Dublin, 1889–1944)

CCM   *Calendar of the Carew manuscripts preserved in the archiepiscopal library at Lambeth, 1515–74*, 6 vols (London, 1867–73)

CDI   *Calendar of documents relating to Ireland, 1171–1307*, ed. H.S. Sweetman and G.F. Handcock, 5 vols (London, 1875–86)

CIRCLE P. Crooks (ed.), *A calendar of Irish chancery letters, c.1244–1509* (http://chancery.tcd.ie/)

CPR   *Calendar of the patent rolls ...* (London, 1901–)

CS   *Chronicum Scotorum: a chronicle of Irish affairs from the earliest times to AD1135, with a supplement containing the*

	events from 1141 to 1150, ed. and trans. W.M. Hennessy (London, 1866)
DIB	*Dictionary of Irish biography*, ed. J. McGuire and J. Quinn, 9 vols (Cambridge, 2009)
FMD	Friends of Medieval Dublin
IHS	*Irish Historical Studies* (Dublin, 1938–)
JRSAI	*Journal of the Royal Society of Antiquaries of Ireland* (Dublin, 1850–)
MD	*The Martyrology of Donegal: a calendar of the saints of Ireland: Félise na Naomh nÉrennach*, trans. J. O'Donovan, ed. J.H. Todd and W. Reeves (Dublin, 1864)
Med. Ire.	S. Duffy (ed.), *Medieval Ireland: an encyclopedia* (New York and Abington, 2005)
NAI	National Archives of Ireland, Dublin
NHI	*A new history of Ireland*, ed. T.W. Moody et al., 9 vols (Oxford, 1976–2005)
OED	Oxford English Dictionary
PRIA	*Proceedings of the Royal Irish Academy* (Dublin, 1836–)
RDKPRI	*Reports of the deputy keeper of the public records in Ireland* (Dublin, 1869–)
RIA	Royal Irish Academy, Dublin
RPH	*Rotulorum patentium et clausorum cancellariae Hiberniae calendarium*, i, part 1, *Hen. II–Hen. VII* (London, 1828)
s.a.	*sub anno, sub annis*
VCH	*The Victoria county history of the counties of England* (London, 1900–)

List of contributors

SPARKY BOOKER is a research associate at the Medieval History Research Centre, Trinity College Dublin.

HOWARD B. CLARKE is Professor Emeritus of Medieval Socio-Economic History at University College Dublin and a member of the Royal Irish Academy.

EDWARD COLEMAN is a lecturer in the School of History and Archives, University College Dublin.

SEÁN DUFFY is Associate Professor of Medieval History and a fellow of Trinity College Dublin as well as chairman of the Friends of Medieval Dublin.

ÁINE FOLEY holds a PhD in medieval history from Trinity College Dublin and is the secretary of the Friends of Medieval Dublin.

POUL HOLM is Trinity Long Room Hub Professor of Humanities at Trinity College Dublin, and director of the Irish Digital Arts and Humanities Structured PhD Programme.

GILLIAN KENNY is a research associate at the Centre for Gender and Women's Studies, Trinity College Dublin.

COLM LENNON is Professor Emeritus of the National University of Ireland, Maynooth.

MARGARET MURPHY is a history lecturer at Carlow College.

MICHAEL O'NEILL is an architectural historian working in Dublin.

CHERIE N. PETERS is a postgraduate student based in the Department of History, Trinity College Dublin.

KATHARINE SIMMS is Fellow Emeritus of Trinity College Dublin.

LINZI SIMPSON is an archaeological consultant and project manager.

CAOIMHE WHELAN holds the Irish Research Council's Daniel O'Connell award in Irish history and is a postgraduate scholar based in the Department of History, Trinity College Dublin.

Introduction and acknowledgments

During Heritage Week 2009, the Friends of Medieval Dublin, a study group keen to promote public interest in the medieval city, conducted a series of guided walking tours around Dublin's medieval centre. Each of these walks was significantly oversubscribed and the passion of the general public for the city's history was palpable. Many of the people who came on the walks were regular attendees at the Friends of Medieval Dublin annual symposium and both they and those who were new to the Friends' events were interested in being given more opportunities to engage with Dublin's past. The Friends were delighted to see such a positive response and resolved to add a free monthly lecture series to their annual calendar of events and entitled it the 'Tales of Medieval Dublin'. Thus, the Tales series and this, the resulting volume, had their origins in the enthusiasm of the people of Dublin for their own history.

The Friends approached Dublin City Council, which was both enthusiastic and generous with its support, offering to host the lectures in the newly renovated Wood Quay Venue and providing promotional materials. This very successful collaboration between the Friends of Medieval Dublin (FMD) and Dublin City Council (DCC) is characteristic of the cooperation between the FMD and DCC that has flourished in the last decade, but belied their earliest, contentious associations with one another. The Friends were in fact formed in 1976 in part as a lobbying group to preserve the important Hiberno-Norse site at Wood Quay that was largely destroyed by the construction of the Dublin Civic Offices (figs 1, 2).[1] The remains of the Hiberno-Norse town wall that ran through Wood Quay were preserved, however, and are now showcased in the Wood Quay Venue, providing a remarkably fitting backdrop for the Tales of Medieval Dublin lectures (figs 3, 4).

The Tales series began in June 2010 and ran for three successful years,

1 Vista of Wood Quay during excavations (© Dublin City Council).

comprising twenty-one lectures. Each tale focused on a different, fascinating inhabitant of the medieval city and these twenty-one lives provided personal insights into many of the most exciting episodes and developments in Dublin's history. The selection of essays in this volume is drawn from these public talks and spans Dublin's extensive medieval past, from its very early pre-Viking roots, all the way up to the early seventeenth century. People from all walks of life are discussed, though there is a particular emphasis on the experiences of the everyday men and women who were the backbone of the Dublin community. Those humble inhabitants, who are often overlooked in histories, find their voice in this volume alongside queens, saints and knights.

In the Saint's Tale, Seán Duffy introduces us to the first ever Dubliner named in a historical source: Saint Bearaidh of the monastery of Duiblinn. Unfortunately, there is reason to distrust the source that records Bearaidh's connection with Dublin and death in the 650s. In a feat of wide-ranging historical detective work, this Tale questions whether Bearaidh was indeed a seventh-century Dublin saint and shows us some of the difficulties

2 Hiberno-Norse wall of Dublin, *c*.1100, *in situ* (© Dublin City Council).

encountered by historians when trying to discover biographical information about individuals from some of the earliest medieval settlements in Dublin. In the second of the Tales, Linzi Simpson reconstructs the life of a young male skeleton, nicknamed Eric, who was found in a furnished Viking burial just south of the black pool (*duiblinn*) that gave Dublin its name. Next, Poul Holm traces the lives of the many unfortunate men and women who were sold on Dublin's early medieval slave market to far-off destinations such as Iceland, Scandinavia, Normandy and the Spanish Caliphate in the Slave's Tale. Howard Clarke's essay, the Mother's Tale, tells the story of Gormlaith, the powerful Irish woman and reputed Jezebel who was the wife of two or possibly three different kings, including the famous Brian Bóruma, and mother of Sigtryggr, or Sitric Silkenbeard, king of Dublin. Turning to the everyday people of the Dublin region, Cherie N. Peters' Farmer's Tale discusses the travails, difficulties and daily lives of the many farmers who provided food and other goods for the medieval town.

3 Wood Quay Venue under construction (© Dublin City Council).

4 Modern Wood Quay Venue (© Dublin City Council).

The late twelfth century saw the advent of the English colony in Ireland and brought great change to Dublin. The challenges and responsibilities faced by those who staffed the local colonial administration, like Thomas de Crumlin, a fourteenth-century tax collector, are discussed by Áine Foley in the Tax Collector's Tale, while Margaret Murphy traces the infamous rise and fall of Nicholas de Clere, archdeacon of Dublin and treasurer of Ireland, in the Archdeacon's Tale. In the Crusader's Tale, Edward Coleman examines the life of William Fitzroger, prior of the order of the Knights Hospitaller in Ireland, who faced conflicting loyalties to his king and his military order. He was summoned to the Holy Land by the master of the Hospitallers, but ordered by the English king to remain in Ireland and help to protect the colony from its Irish enemies. Gillian Kenny's Wife's Tale uncovers the everyday life of a high-born medieval woman in Dublin using a close analysis of the contents of her will. In the Notary's Tale, Caoimhe Whelan traces the life of James Yonge, a fifteenth-century notary who was commissioned by the earl of Ormond to create a Hiberno-Middle English version of the pseudo-Aristotelian *Secreta secretorum*.

The final decades of the Middle Ages, with the Reformation and Kildare rebellion, provided new challenges for Dublin and its inhabitants. Colm Lennon describes the difficulties that James Stanihurst, father of the more famous Richard, faced as a sixteenth-century speaker of the Irish House of Commons in the Man of Law's Tale. In the Knight's Tale, Sparky Booker tells the story of Christopher St Lawrence, seventh baron of Howth, whose tumultuous public and personal life led to his trial and imprisonment for the death of his daughter. Finally, Katharine Simms looks at the life of a bardic poet, Maoilín Óg Mac Bruidhea, who resided in the newly established Trinity College (founded in 1592) as he assisted the project to translate the gospels into Irish in the early seventeenth century. These fascinating tales, which span almost a millennium, act not just as a history of the city, but also as a window into the day-to-day lives of lesser-known medieval men and women.

The lecture series and this resulting volume would not have been possible without the help of a number of dedicated individuals and each of them has our sincerest thanks. Ruth Johnson, city archaeologist, and Charles Duggan, heritage officer, were instrumental in the realization of this lecture series, and provided a spectacular venue as well as funds for promotion as part of the Dublin City Heritage Plan. They have also provided a generous subvention for the present volume, for which we are extremely grateful. The distinguished individuals who launched the three series of the Tales, MEP Emer Costello, then lord mayor, President Michael D. Higgins, then senator, and Senator David Norris, were generous with their support and we owe them a debt of gratitude. Katrina Bouchier designed the brilliant poster series for the lectures. We would like to thank Howard Clarke and Seán Duffy in particular from the Friends of Medieval Dublin for all of their help with the series and this volume. Grace O'Keeffe was an integral part in making the first series in 2010 such a success and her help in the following years was immeasurable. We would like to thank all of the Friends who helped to organize and attended the lectures, particularly Caoimhe Whelan, Peter Crooks, Áine Foley, Sheila Dooley, Mary-Therese Byrne, Patrick Herbage and Fidelma Yore. We would also like to thank John Downey and all the staff at Wood Quay for making the venue available to us, recording podcasts and preparing the space in advance of each lecture. We owe Donal Ó hUallachain a huge thank you for allowing us to take over his radio show, *Looking Back*, on Dublin City FM the week before most of the lectures. We would also like to thank all of the staff at St Audoen's, St Patrick's Cathedral and Christ Church Cathedral for being so helpful in promoting the series, along with Con Manning, Rachel Moss, Ruth Sheehy, Theresa O'Byrne, Helena King, Petra Schnabel, the National Museum of Ireland, the British Library, the Huntington Library, the Royal Irish Academy, the National Library of Ireland and Dublinia for their assistance with images. Lastly, we would like to thank everyone who attended the lecture series and, particularly, the many audience members who encouraged us to bring these lectures together in the present volume.

Sparky Booker and Cherie N. Peters

Dublin, 4 July 2014

The Saint's Tale

SEÁN DUFFY

We know very little about human settlement at Dublin before Vikings established a military camp there in the ninth century. There was a ford over the Liffey at a place called Áth Cliath ('ford of hurdles'), but we are not sure where that was and whether there was any population centre associated with it.[1] There was certainly an ecclesiastical presence in the area, possibly near a 'black pool' on the River Poddle, which may be the *Duiblinn* from which the name Dublin is derived. The large early Christian cemetery discovered nearby at the church of St Michael le Pole, in the southern suburbs of the later Viking town, is incontestable evidence of this ecclesiastical presence (although we have never been provided with precise dates for the burials) and it may be the pre-Viking church of Duiblinn.[2]

The subject of this tale is an individual who purportedly oversaw the monastery of Duiblinn in its earliest days. He was called Bearaidh (presumably, in Old Irish, Beraid), and – assuming he ever actually existed – has one other great claim to fame: he is apparently Dublin's first saint and predeceased its most famous saint, St Laurence O'Toole, by more than half a millennium. There is a single reference to Bearaidh in an Irish annalistic compilation, his death being mentioned under the year AD650 in the printed editions and some manuscripts of the Annals of the Four Masters (AFM) (fig. 1.1).[3] The same entry calls him a saint and tells us that he was abbot of the monastic site at 'Duiblinn': '*S. Bearaidh abb Duibhlinne do ecc* [St Bearaidh, abbot of Duiblinn, died]'. That, six words in total, is the full extent of the information provided and it is not much to go on.

The lateness of the evidence for Bearaidh is a worry. The Annals of the Four Masters, compiled in the 1630s from earlier materials, is among the

1.1 Annals of the Four Masters: Bearaidh's entry appears at the end of the first block of text (RIA MS C iii 3, fo. 256r) (by permission of the Royal Irish Academy © RIA).

latest of the genre. To make matters worse, the Bearaidh entry occurs in only one of the two autograph manuscripts of the text, that in the Royal Irish Academy (RIA) called RIA MS C iii 3, and even here it is in the form of an addition to the main text at the end of the entry for AD650. Bernadette Cunningham is the foremost expert on the Four Masters and pointed out to me that the hand is not that of any of the five regular members of the scribal team that put the annals together, and that the Bearaidh entry is likely to be a later insertion added after the rest of the work had been completed, possibly in the eighteenth century.[4]

There is another possible indicator of lateness. AFM's chief compiler, Mícheál Ó Cléirigh, completed another work, a collection of saints' feastdays called the Martyrology of Donegal,[5] just before or in tandem with AFM, and saints whose year of death occurs in AFM tend also to have their feast-day listed in the martyrology.[6] But Bearaidh is not mentioned in the latter – at least using that form of his name (to which we shall return) – suggesting that he was not known to the Four Masters in the 1630s. Incidentally, when AFM provides a saint's obit, it will frequently supply the feast-day also, since the information generally originated in a calendar of feast-days (and was probably just assigned to a year in the annals roughly where the compiler estimated it belonged). But the Bearaidh entry in AFM gives his *year* of death but not his feast-*day*, which suggests that the source of the information was not a calendar of saints (again, a subject to which we shall return).

If, therefore, the Four Masters knew nothing of the name Bearaidh, and this brief mention of him was added to the RIA autograph manuscript (RIA MS C.iii.3) by someone into whose possession it came at a later date, it may be worth tracing the manuscript's later history to try to see when exactly Bearaidh enters the picture. The manuscript was part of a presentation set of AFM given at its completion in 1636 to the project's patron Fearghal Ó Gadhra, lord of Coolavin in Sligo. Perhaps the first scholar in a position to make additions to it was no less a figure than the renowned Dubhaltach Mac Fhirbhisigh, who made use of it when compiling his 'Great Book of Genealogies' in Galway in 1649.[7] In the 1650s it turns up in the possession of a certain Henry Bourke of Co. Galway,[8] and was almost certainly used by that other great scholar Ruaidhri Ó Flaithbheartaigh (Roderic O'Flaherty), who was a protégé of Mac Fhirbhisigh and has numerous citations from AFM in his famous work *Ogygia; or, A chronological account of Irish events: collected from very ancient documents*, published in 1685.[9] It is rumoured that the manuscript was brought to the Continent by one of the Wild Geese after 1691, but the next certain trace of it is in Dublin when it surfaces in 1724 in the possession of an avid book-collector, John Conry. It returned to Connacht in 1731 when the Conry's library was sold to the Roman Catholic archbishop of Tuam, Brian/Bernard O'Gara, perhaps a grandson of the Fearghal Ó Gadhra who had been AFM's original patron.

By this stage Charles O'Conor (1710–91) of Belanagare, Co. Roscommon, had already begun collecting manuscripts,[10] and he acquired our manuscript from Archbishop O'Gara in 1734. He consulted it extensively while writing his most famous work, *Dissertations on the antient history of Ireland*, which he began publishing in 1748.[11] O'Conor was arguably the greatest Gaelic antiquary of the eighteenth century,[12] intensely interested in AFM, and he made numerous annotations to the manuscript (often on matters concerning his own ancestors, the Uí Chonchobhair kings of Connacht). Following O'Conor's death in 1791, his manuscripts were acquired by George Grenville, the first marquess of Buckingham, and our AFM manuscript was brought to his home in Stowe in Buckinghamshire, where it was agreed that O'Conor's grandson, Revd Charles O'Conor, would become librarian.[13] The latter too was a Gaelic scholar, though not a patch on his grandfather, and he soon began work on his edition of AFM, which appeared in 1826 as part of his multi-volume *Rerum Hibernicarum scriptores veteres* (1814–28).[14] Under the events of the year AD650, O'Conor includes the entry relating to Bearaidh, '*S. Beraidh abb. Duibhlinne do ecc*', which he translates (into Latin) as 'S. Beradius Abbas Dubliniensis obiit'.

It seems, therefore, that the Bearaidh addition to RIA MS C iii 3 was made at some unknown date after its completion in the 1630s and before the appearance of O'Conor's 1826 edition. We can narrow the date more closely. During the course of the eighteenth century, when it was in the possession of the elder Charles O'Conor, our manuscript was copied at least three times. On the first occasion, a transcript was made in 1734–5 by the scribe Aodh Ó Maolmhuaidh for the Dublin-based medic Dr John Fergus, a friend of O'Conor's with a similar interest in books and manuscripts:[15] this is preserved in Trinity College Dublin, now TCD MS 1300 (formerly H.2.9–10). This transcript does not contain the Bearaidh addition, which was presumably therefore not yet in the original.

The second transcript was required when, in 1763, O'Conor wrote to the eminent scholar of legal history Francis Stoughton Sullivan, of Trinity College, proposing that they collaborate on an edition of AFM, a project in which the latter had long been interested. Dr Sullivan therefore commissioned the well-known Co. Monaghan scribe Muiris Ó Gormáin to make a copy and to produce a translation (although by 1766 Sullivan had died and the project was aborted).[16] The transcript is still preserved in Trinity, now TCD MS 1279 (formerly H.1.3–5), but there is no reference to Bearaidh in this copy either. This is fairly solid proof that the Bearaidh entry had not yet been entered into the original, RIA MS C iii 3.

The third transcript *does* contain the reference to Bearaidh, however, in a hand identical to the rest of the text. It was made in 1781 for the famous Chevalier O'Gorman, and is now RIA MS 23 F 2–3. The printed catalogue of Irish manuscripts in the RIA, following an earlier identification by Eugene O'Curry, names the scribe as an individual called Brennan/Brannan,[17] but Nollaig Ó Muraíle has recently identified him as a young man called Martin Hughes.[18] What is more, if one compares the hand of this 1781 transcript with that which penned the Bearaidh insertion into the mother-text (RIA MS C iii 3), they are apparently one and the same.

To summarize the situation, in Charles O'Conor's printed edition of the Annals of the Four Masters published in 1826 there is a reference to the death of Bearaidh, abbot of Duiblinn, under the year AD650. But that piece of information was not known to the Four Masters. It was added into their annals as late as 1781 by one Martin Hughes. Where Hughes got the information we simply cannot say. We know very little about him but what little we do know suggests that he did not unearth it himself: the source of the information was almost certainly his employer, Charles O'Conor of Belanagare. In a letter to his son written on 6 April 1781, O'Conor stated that

> I trained up a little boy, one Martin Hughes, to transcribe Irish annals for Chevalier O'Gorman on being certain that the latter would give some consideration for the task. I advanced that boy a guinea, which the chevalier advanced me cheerfully together with two guineas in addition, which I shall remit by Paddy Hart or some other safe hand. It will be a relief to that poor boy's parents.

From this it is clear that Martin Hughes was merely a young amanuensis for the then 71-year-old O'Conor. Indeed, just a matter of weeks earlier the latter had written to O'Gorman again referring to Hughes as the 'boy I have instructed in Irish', but adding that he 'is far from being sufficiently instructed. He is yet but barely fit for a facsimile, for transcribing what is laid before him without understanding it'.[19] We have to assume therefore that Charles O'Conor of Belanagare located the Bearaidh reference and asked Martin Hughes to add it to AFM *s.a.* 650.

Given O'Conor's credentials as a scholar, that is some consolation, but where might he have obtained the reference to Bearaidh? One possibility suggests itself. A lifelong acquaintance of his was John Carpenter (Seán Mac an tSaoir), who would become Roman Catholic archbishop of Dublin in 1770.[20] About 1727, when in his late teens, Charles O'Conor had been sent to Dublin to study, and linked up with the Ó Neachtain circle of Gaelic scholars.[21] John Carpenter was not born until 1729 but would soon also receive an education in the Irish language and develop an interest in Gaelic antiquarian studies at Tadhg Ó Neachtain's school and in the process become a friend of O'Conor. John Carpenter was transcribing his own manuscripts by the time he was in his mid-teens and in later years he and O'Conor would regularly exchange manuscripts. One of Carpenter's, RIA MS 23 A 8, written in 1746, is a prayer book in Irish that contains a calendar of Irish saints. And this list of saints includes Bearaidh. His feast-day is given as 8 May, and he is described as '*Bearaidhe, ep. Athacliath* [Bearaidh(e), bishop of Dublin]'.[22] It is possible that O'Conor found the reference to Bearaidh here – although there are obvious differences in the information provided, which we shall return to – and chose to insert a mention of him into AFM *s.a.* 650. At the very least, Archbishop Carpenter's calendar of saints provides a small amount of corroboration of the existence of Bearaidh – whoever else may have been responsible, he is not a figment of the imagination of Charles O'Conor of Belanagare.

So Bearaidh was a man whom Charles O'Conor believed to have been a saint, an abbot who presided over a monastery at 'Duiblinn', and who died on some unknown date in the year AD650. John Carpenter also knew

Bearaidh as a saint, but thought he was a bishop rather than an abbot, ruled 'Áth Cliath' rather than 'Duiblinn', and he did not know the year of Bearaidh's death but knew the date was 8 May. How do we reconcile these differences?

Assuming for a moment that he was a real person, there would be no great difficulty in the fact that one has Bearaidh as an abbot and the other as a bishop: Colmán Etchingham, for instance, has noted that, of the 204 bishops recorded in the annals between AD750 and AD1000, no fewer than 94 also bear Latin titles like *abbas* or *princeps* or their Irish vernacular equivalents *ap* and *airchinnech*.[23] Bearaidh would therefore have been a bishop and also an *abbas*, but not necessarily an abbot in the sense in which we use the term. Instead, the point being made was simply that he was head of the church of Duiblinn (by the early modern period, Áth Cliath served as a synonym for Duiblinn and the original distinction between the two sites was lost).[24] Both O'Conor and Carpenter describe him as a saint and the probability is that they meant a saint in the way that, say, St Ciarán or St Kevin was a saint; that is, the founder or an eminent early head of a major church like Clonmacnoise or Glendalough. They therefore imagined Bearaidh as a man who died in AD650, presumably elderly or middle-aged, having founded his church, say, a decade or two earlier.

If any credence was to be given to this suggestion, it might just be relevant that the Annals of Ulster record the foundation in AD635 of the church of Rechru,[25] most probably on Lambay off the coast of north Co. Dublin. AFM adds that the founder was St Ségéne, the fifth abbot of the great Columban church of Iona.[26] It is just possible, therefore, that the supposed establishment of Duiblinn around this time fits in with a pattern of church foundation in the Dublin area, possibly associated with evangelizing activity by churchmen from what is now Scotland. We might cite, for instance, Kilmahuddrick near Clondalkin, which is Cell Mo-Chudric, the church of St Cuthbert (d. 687), Aidan of Iona's most illustrious successor as bishop of Lindisfarne. Although there cannot be any substance to traditions that assert that Kilmahuddrick acquired its name because it was Cuthbert's place of birth,[27] the name has an almost identical parallel in Kirkcudbright

(Cell Chudric) on the south coast of Galloway and indicates some kind of early connection between this part of Scotland and the Dublin region. Portmarnock in north Dublin is Port M'Ernóc, the harbour of St M'Ernóc, otherwise known as Erníne or Ernán, who may be the same saint from whom Kilmarnock in East Ayrshire and Inchmarnock, an island in the Firth of Clyde, get their names.[28]

With this in mind it may be worth noting that in South Knapdale, on the west coast of Kintyre, there is an early church site called Kilberry (Cill Bhearaidh), which *might* – it is a remote enough possibility – be the church of our Bearaidh, if he was a real person.[29] It is normally – and perhaps rightly – assumed to be associated with St Berach, that better-known holy man who has given his name to Kilbarry and Termonbarry in Co. Roscommon and to Kilberry, north of Navan, Co. Meath, and perhaps also to Kilbarrack, north-east of Dublin.[30] Given their proximity, one might have thought the Bearaidh who allegedly ruled Duiblinn and the Berach/Barróc remembered in Kilbarrack are one and the same, but there is a problem in making such an equation. The feast-day of the latter is 15 February.[31] As we saw above, however, in Archbishop Carpenter's calendar of saints, Bearaidh's feast-day is given as 8 May. It would seem, therefore, that we are dealing with two different saints.

Bearing in mind Bearaidh's supposed feast-day, one possible line of enquiry is to look for another saint whose feast is 8 May, to see if Bearaidh might be lurking there under a different name. Pádraig Ó Riain has called my attention to the fact that in the Martyrology of Donegal, which, as mentioned above, Mícheál Ó Cléirigh and the Four Masters were compiling contemporaneously with AFM,[32] under 8 May there occurs the feast of '*Uuiro, ardepscop Atha Cliath, AD750* (Wiro, archbishop of Dublin, AD750)'.[33] The coincidence of these two saints, both bishops of Dublin and both being celebrated on 8 May, is of course too great: they are evidently one and the same. And although the martyrology's 'Uuiro' and Carpenter's 'Bearaidhe' at first sight seem miles apart, if Uuiro is pronounced *Viro* or *Wiro* and Bearaidhe is lenited (to become 'Bhearaidhe') and pronounced something like *Veri* or *Weri*, one can see how they might be the same man.

Regarding St Wiro – better known as the patron of the Dutch city of Roermond – and his association with Dublin as posited in Ó Cléirigh's martyrology, he is one of a number of such elusive characters, who have an increasing tendency to crop up in the works of Counter-Reformation hagiographers (some of them associated, like Ó Cléirigh, with Louvain). For instance, his fellow Donegal-man and Franciscan friar, John Colgan, in his famous book on Irish saints called *Triadis Thaumaturgæ*, published in Louvain in 1647, states that St Livinus of Ghent (d. 657?) had been bishop of Dublin, although on what basis it is not known and it seems doubtful.[34] An even less likely candidate is St Disibod (d. 700?), from whom the monastery of Disibodenberg in the Rhineland takes its name (and where his biographer, the revered Hildegard of Bingen, spent much of her life): the earliest statement that Disibod was 'borne in Ireland, and a monke of the order of S. Benedict, was ordayned bishop of Dublin in the same kingdome', seems to be Fr John Wilson's *English martyrologe*, published in St Omer in 1608, and is greatly to be doubted.[35] Best known of these early saints is the man after whom St Rombold's Cathedral in the Belgian city of Mechelen is named; reputedly Irish, the earliest reference I have found to Rombold/Rumoldus having left 'the archbishopric of Dublin (*archiepiscopatu Dublinensi*)' to evangelize in the Low Countries is in the *Indiculus sanctorum Belgii*, published in Louvain in 1572 by a theologian of its university, Jan Vermeulen (Joannes Molanus),[36] which inspires very little confidence.

Therefore, when the eminent Anglo-Irish historian Sir James Ware published in Dublin in 1665 his *De praesulibus Hiberniae commentarius*, which has a chapter on the history of the bishops of Dublin, he was not impressed by these pronouncements as to the existence of early incumbents of the see and, mentioning them in passing, states that he will begin instead with Dúnán (Donatus), the eleventh-century bishop whose historicity seems beyond doubt.[37] But in 1739 and 1746, Walter Harris, who had married Ware's granddaughter, published a two-volume English translation of Ware's works, with much additional material. In his chapter on the bishops of Dublin, while remaining somewhat sceptical about their historicity, Harris decided to give brief accounts of a number of these supposed early prelates, including Livinus, Disibod and Rumoldus.

To them he added the St Wiro we mentioned above, whose feast-day is 8 May.[38] Harris says he acquired most of his information about Wiro from *De probatis sanctorum vitis*, first published in Cologne in the 1570s by a member of its Catholic Carthusian community Lorenz Sauer (Laurentius Surius), an expanded edition of which appeared in 1617–18, but although this work has an account of Wiro's life and declares that he was Irish, it does not mention Dublin.[39] Harris acquired further information about Wiro – the fact that he ended his days in Roermond – from Vermeulen's *Indiculus sanctorum Belgii* (1572), but, while the latter too has Wiro as Irish, neither does it mention Dublin.[40] Where, then, did Harris acquire the belief that Wiro was bishop of Dublin? Since, on the following page, he cites Mícheál Ó Cléirigh's Martyrology of Donegal – in which, as we have seen, under 8 May there occurs the feast of '*Uuiro, ardepscop Atha Cliath, AD750* (Wiro, archbishop of Dublin, AD750)'[41] – we can assume this was his source.

To summarize our tale: in Dublin in 1739 a book was published – Walter Harris' English translation of the works of Sir James Ware – which tells us of the death of St Wiro, bishop of Dublin, on 8 May. Seven years later, in the same city, the young John Carpenter put together a list of Irish saints that included, under 8 May, '*Bearaidhe, ep. Athacliath* (Bearaidhe, bishop of Dublin)'.[42] More than likely, the name 'Bearaidhe' is Carpenter's attempt to render 'Wiro', and more than likely he first read of St Wiro in Harris' *Ware*. But we are still left with the problem of how Bearaidh(e) ended up in AFM under AD650. The source of this is straightforward. The Martyrology of Donegal had, as we have seen, given St Wiro's death as AD750. But Walter Harris rejected this date because, as noted, he tended to rely on material found in Sauer's *De probatis sanctorum vitis*: here, St Wiro's death is given as AD650.[43]

In other words, after 1739, following the appearance of Harris' *Ware* – which rapidly became required reading for Irish antiquarians – the date AD650 became attached for the first time in an Irish source to a bishop of Dublin, bearing a name, Wiro, which people like John Carpenter thought might be a Latinization of an Irish name like Bearaidh(e). Carpenter was a friend of Charles O'Conor of Belanagare. In 1781, O'Conor had his young amanuensis Martin Hughes make an insertion into his manuscript of the Annals of the Four Masters. It reads: '*S. Bearaidh abb Duibhlinne do ecc* [St Bearaidh, abbot of Duiblinn, died]'.[44] It was inserted under the year AD650, and this was done almost certainly because that is where St Wiro's death is placed in Harris' *Ware*. Surely St Bearaidh(e) of Duiblinn is St Wiro of Roermond. And surely, therefore, it is highly unlikely that he ever had anything to do with Dublin?

POSTSCRIPT

What then of the church of which Bearaidh was said to be head: did the pre-Viking monastery of Duiblinn actually exist? The only evidence seems to be preserved in the Annals of Ulster – which tend to be more reliable than AFM – which record the death of a man called Siadal in AD790, described as abbot or head of the church of Duiblinn (*abbas Duiblinne*). If Bearaidh never existed, perhaps this Siadal did, and perhaps the inclusion of Siadal's obit in a list of seven kings and nobles who died in that year – among them the church-heads of Glendalough and Downpatrick – is evidence that the pre-Viking church of Duiblinn was indeed a prestigious establishment.

The Skeleton's Tale

LINZI SIMPSON

In 2003 a large archaeological excavation at South Great George's Street, Dublin, revealed the remains of a ninth-century Viking settlement and cemetery, at the confluence of the rivers Poddle and Liffey. This is the earliest evidence of Viking habitation found in Dublin to date (fig. 2.1, pl. 1).[1]

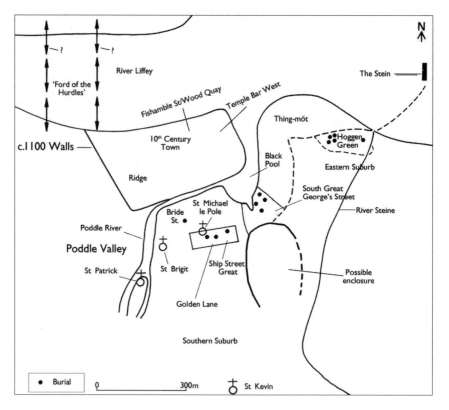

2.1 Map of medieval Dublin, showing locations of Viking furnished burials.

The findings suggest a defended settlement, with traces of buildings, hearths and pits – the usual indicators of occupation – but also the furnished graves of four young men, buried in and around the settlement features. These individuals were quickly identified as young males by an osteologist, Laureen Buckley, and their age and sex suggested that they were likely to be young Viking warriors. This is bolstered by the fact that at least one, possibly two, were interred with militaristic weaponry.[2] One of these young men, nicknamed 'Eric' by excavators, is the skeleton of this tale. The location of his and his fellow warrior's burials was something of a surprise, lying some distance south of the Liffey's banks in the low-lying Poddle valley and set on the southern edge of a deep tidal pool on the Poddle river. This sheltered body of water may well be the Duiblinn or 'black pool' referred to in the documentary sources and the reputed origin of the place-name Dublin. It is now the Dubhlinn gardens at the back of Dublin Castle (pl. 1).

The location was in complete contrast to the previously discovered remnants of early Viking Dublin. These centred on the fortified embanked settlement or *dún*, dated from the late ninth century at least, which was perched on a high ridge just to the north-west of the black pool, fronting onto the south bank of the Liffey (fig. 2.1). Extensive excavations within this historic core, in and around Christ Church, High Street, Castle Street, Werburgh Street, Winetavern Street, Wood Quay and Temple Bar West, have revealed rare anaerobic (airless) ground conditions, which have ensured the survival of the earthen and timber defences, houses, outhouses, workshops, paths and even latrines that all lie perfectly preserved beneath the rubble of the early modern period.[3]

The new pool-side settlement at South Great George's Street has added another dimension to what was proposed archaeologically in the past for the evolution of Dublin. This site was probably earlier than the ridge site, with evidence of settlement certainly by the mid-ninth century, if not before. The attraction may have been the pool itself, where Viking ships could be safely moored in the calm and protected waters. This, then, was one of the first places at which the Vikings established a foothold in

Dublin, their commitment to their new land being represented by the graves of four young men, buried within their new settlement. They buried these men ritualistically, furnishing their graves with personal items and weaponry. This type of burial is specifically associated with the Scandinavians and was at its peak in the ninth century. Most importantly, this ritual interment appears to have been the preserve of high-born individuals, rather than the ordinary rank-and-file, and was also an indicator of 'social class', as older men, unlikely to be warriors at their time of death, and women with personal objects other than weaponry were also buried this way.

These types of grave are well known in Dublin, where an extraordinary number have been found to date. Dublin has produced at least seventy-five such furnished graves, which represents, remarkably, one quarter of all

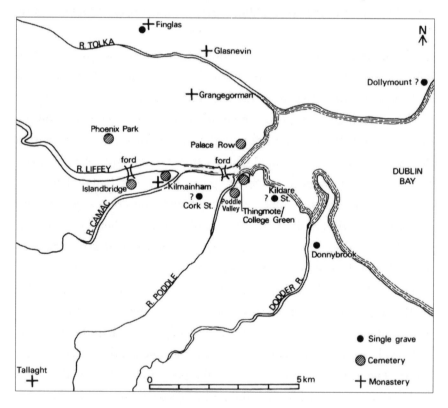

2.2 Viking furnished burials in the Liffey valley.

known male graves containing weapons in Ireland and Britain combined, as calculated by Stephen Harrison.[4] For once, the historical and archaeological evidence agree: Dublin was flooded with young Scandinavian warriors in the ninth century, many of whom died or were slain on campaign and buried in Dublin along the flood plain of the lower Liffey (fig. 2.2).

This essay attempts to sketch the life of one of these young Viking men, nicknamed 'Eric' during excavations. These warriors are likely to have come to this small island, then on the edge of the known world, spurred on, no doubt, by tales of the fortunes made by their kinsmen. Unfortunately, a different fate awaited our warrior, since his young age at the time of death suggests that he met a violent end. His untimely death, however, provides us with an opportunity to use new scientific processes to reveal details of his everyday life, from the cradle to the grave (fig. 2.3).

2.3 'Eric', warrior skeleton F196 and associated grave-goods *in situ* at South Great George's Street.

HISTORICAL BACKGROUND

Students of the Viking period in Ireland are fortunate to have at their disposal the Irish annals, the contemporary monastic records, which provide a graphic, if terse, literary narrative of an invading force that dominated the political scene from their arrival in the late eighth century to their infamous defeat by Brian Bóruma at the Battle of Clontarf in 1014.[5] These Irish sources record only too well the impact of the Vikings when they first appeared off the Irish coast in the mid-790s and they faithfully chart wave upon wave of young Viking warriors that arrived in Ireland in huge numbers and the terrifying period that followed, typified by savage raids, plundering, killing and, perhaps the most frightening of all, the taking of hostages and slaves. From the beginning, Ireland must have been viewed as an untapped resource, an easy target, rich in easily portable ecclesiastical booty. Here was an island of numerous small kingdoms and with a population totally unprepared for the particular water-borne Viking 'smash and grab' brand of warfare. The pattern of their raiding and their mastery of the water ensured that Viking raiding parties could exploit the internal waterway systems and penetrate the interior quickly, as the annals record.

But during this first phase – often characterized as comprising merely of 'hit and run' raids – the invaders could not have been blind to the settlement potential of this rich and fertile land, with its soft climate, in sharp contrast to their homelands, particularly Norway. Viking interest in some sort of settlement along the eastern coastline was demonstrated early by the formation of camps at Áth Cliath/Duiblinn at Dublin and Linn Duachaill, now identified as Annagassan, Co. Louth. The topographical location of both these sites, boasting easy access to the sea, was obviously pivotal to the decision of the raiding Vikings to over-winter in both locations in 841. The Irish annalists used the term *longphort* or 'ship camp' to describe these new settlements at the mouths of the Liffey and the Glyde rivers. The decision not to return home at the end of the campaigning season represented a seismic shift towards permanency and a definite move away from what must have been simply transitory raiding camps, and the significance of the settlements was not lost on the annalists, who recorded these alarming developments. In addition to their coastal location, Annagassan and Dublin had something else in common: both are recorded in the annals as monastic sites. The very fact that their affairs were noted by monastic authors signifies that they were ecclesiastical centres of some significance prior to the arrival of the Vikings. Thus, at both of these sites organized settlement already existed, with a resident population that had to be overcome. Most importantly, these sites also had an infrastructure, in the form of cleared farmland, trading routes, roads, livestock and food stores.

FURNISHED VIKING BURIALS IN DUBLIN

Perversely, despite the rich and varied documentary sources detailing the activities of the Vikings in Dublin in the ninth century, until recently very little has been known, in terms of archaeology, about this earliest phase of contact. The excavations by the National Museum of Ireland in and around the historic core at Christ Church revealed the rich remains of the Viking settlement that the settlers called Dyflinn, but there was little diagnostic evidence to suggest the presence of the historically recorded Viking warriors based there in the ninth century (fig. 2.1). In fact, the main body of evidence for this early phase came not from Dublin, but from Kilmainham/Islandbridge, 2km upstream from the Liffey-Poddle confluence, where the spectacular remains of fifty-five furnished Viking burials, in two clusters, were discovered in the nineteenth and early twentieth century (fig. 2.2).[6] But in this period other furnished graves were found farther downstream, towards the mouth of the Liffey, on both sides of the river. On the northern side, the discovery of furnished burials in the Phoenix Park and in and around Parnell Square suggests at least two grave-fields or cemeteries on this side of the river, while, on the southern side, individual graves have been found at Cork Street, Bride Street and Kildare Street. There was also a possible cemetery at Hoggen Green, now College Green, denoted by burial mounds, two of which survived into the seventeenth century. Then in 2001, unexpectedly, during excavations by the writer of very limited medieval deposits at Ship Street Great, another very truncated male skeleton was found, which was quickly identified as a Viking furnished grave.

Unfortunately, all that survived of the Ship Street Great burial was the upper torso of a young male on his back, mostly the neck area, but enough survived to reveal that he had several items around his neck – a bead, a delicate silver finger ring, a small twisted silver ring and a square piece of corroded iron, possibly originally decorative. The clinching detail was another fragment of iron, which, on X-ray, revealed the typical herring-bone construction of the pattern-welded sword that originally accompanied the warrior.

The findings at Ship Street Great were bolstered two years later in 2003 when the remains of Viking settlement were found at South Great George's Street spread out along the southern edge of the pool. The archaeological evidence suggests that Viking boats were moored here, since ship rivets were found in the gravel layers that would have been the bottom of the pool. The settlement was delineated by two successive palisades and at least one bank, and most of the evidence was preserved in the boulder clay, where numerous post-holes, hearths, ditches, spreads of animal bone and rubbish pits were found. In and among these features were the badly damaged graves of four young men, clustered within a small area measuring only 25m square (out of a site measuring 100m by 60m) and cut into the boulder clay. Undisturbed boulder clay is the earliest level on site, pre-dating occupation levels.

The subject of this essay – 'Eric', numbered F196 – was the first burial discovered at South Great George's Street. The initial indication that something was unusual about this part of the excavation was what appeared to be an iron pipe projecting from the ground and presumed to be origi-nally an intrusive artefact, most likely modern. On excavation, however, the partial remains of a human skeleton – Eric – were exposed lying beneath. The 'pipe' was quickly identified as the remains of an iron shield boss and arm-guard, all that survived of the timber shield that was originally laid across the abdomen of this young adult male during burial. This, then, appeared to be a furnished Viking grave, of a type well known in Dublin.

The location was of great interest because of its close proximity to the Ship Street Great burial, raising the possibility that both were linked and that they, in turn, could be linked to the antiquarian find of a furnished grave in Bride Street farther west. Thus, the picture that began to emerge was of a linear pattern of burial along the Poddle valley, stretching from Bride Street in the west to the pool in the east. The accuracy of this picture was quickly confirmed by the discovery of three additional warriors at the South Great George's Street site. The density of burial suggests that this area was a cemetery or grave-field on a similar model to the great cemeteries of Kilmainham/Islandbridge.

Of the other three burials found at the site, only one (F598) was relatively intact. He was a young, strong, big-boned and muscular man, aged between 17 and 25 years, with no weaponry, but several personal items including a comb, a bone pin with an animal head (a hare?), an unidentified metal object and a blade. The second burial (F223) had been badly disturbed by later features, but, while little more than a fragmented torso survived, there was enough to establish that he was a male, aged between 17 and 20 years, and probably buried with a shield. This was suggested by the discovery of two iron rivets and five pieces of iron in his grave. These rivets are identical to those found in the shield boss associated with Eric's burial (see below). The third burial (F342) was also badly damaged, but enough of the skeleton survived to determine that he was a male, aged less than 25 years, and of relatively short stature, measuring only 1.66m in height.

The conclusion that these burials formed part of a cemetery in and around the pool was spectacularly corroborated in 2005 when excavations by Edmond O'Donovan, at the church site of St Michael le Pole, identified not only what may be the early Christian cemetery of the monastery of Duiblinn but also four outlying burials, two of which were definitely Viking furnished graves (fig. 2.1).[7] One was a young male of very high status. This is evident from the plethora of grave-goods buried with him, including an iron spearhead, a copper-alloy belt-buckle, an iron knife, a strap-end and two lead weights (although no sword). Even more exciting was the second burial, since this contained the first woman found in the Poddle valley buried in the 'warrior tradition'. She was also clearly a high-status individual, buried with a particularly fine bone buckle. Two additional graves are likely to have been Viking, as they were both males, one older, one younger, and the latter was located less than 10m away from the Ship Street Great burial.

THE VIKING WARRIOR CALLED ERIC

The survival of Eric's grave was nothing short of miraculous, since the area in which it was found, to the rear of properties along South Great George's Street, was developed extensively from the late seventeenth century onwards, with post-medieval features such as ditches and basements cutting right down to the Viking deposits beneath. As a result, very little survived at this end of the site, and the boulder clay was exposed when the post-medieval layers and structures were removed. Significant damage to the grave was also caused by a seventeenth-century ditch, which removed the legs and truncated the body's right side, while additional disturbance was caused by a deposit of dumped brick. The grave was cut into the natural yellow boulder-clay level, but was within an area previously occupied, since the grave-cut partially truncated an earlier oblong rubbish pit (F198). This burial, then, had been opened in an area that was settled and occupied, as were at least two other burials. Curiously, the skeleton was at a similar level to the settlement features immediately west, which may suggest that originally the grave was not dug deep into the ground, but rather sealed by a mound of clay or cairn of stones, as was used for a furnished burial at a Viking site of a similar date at Woodstown, Co. Waterford, where the grave lies just 20m outside the enclosure.

Eric's skeleton was on its back, orientated north-east/south-west with the head to the north-east, unlike Christian burials, which are almost always orientated east–west with the head to the west (figs 2.4, 2.5). A layer of

2.4 Excavation of Eric's skeleton in the laboratory.

charcoal was identified beneath the skeleton along his left side (see below). The left arm was flexed at a 90° angle across the abdomen, but the right arm was clearly out of position since the forearm was crossed over the upper arm, suggesting that it was severed from the body. The legs and right side of the skeleton had been removed by post-medieval building activity, but despite the poor preservation Laureen Buckley, the osteologist, established the crucial facts almost immediately. The narrow sciatic notch in the pelvis suggested to Buckley that this was a male. Further examination of the largest bone of the hip (the ilium) indicated that he was between 25 and 29 years of age. Buckley was also able to estimate his height at 1.71m, based on the length of the upper arm (humerus); this was an average height for this time. Thus, the first skeleton found with a shield on his chest at South Great George's Street, on examination, fitted very neatly the expected profile for a young Viking warrior.

Overall, the skeleton was in poor condition. All that remained of the

2.5 Drawing the burial on site at South Great George's Street.

skull was part of the mandible or lower jaw and seven teeth, but his spine fared slightly better since six lower thoracic and five lumbar vertebrae survived, all in relatively good condition. The left side of the pelvis was relatively intact, while fragments of the sacrum (the lower back) also survived. Six lower ribs from the left side and four from the right were in position but in very poor condition, as was part of the left shoulder (scapula). The upper arm survived, although both ends were damaged. The lower left arm was *in situ* but one end had been removed during the construction of the seventeenth-century ditch. The right arm was completely out of alignment, as mentioned previously, and was in poor condition. There were very few hand bones – in fact only four, which came from the fingers and wrists, were recovered.

Eric's badly damaged skeleton and the fragmentary remains of his weapons are all that survive of this young Viking warrior, who was afforded a furnished burial befitting his aristocratic status, with all the pomp and ceremony that surely attached to this burial rite. But the shattered torso can reveal hidden details about his life and childhood, providing some sort of a window into his past. His seven surviving teeth were examined and the evidence of some erosion is suggestive of serious childhood nutritional deficiency sometime between the age of one and five. This young man experienced a brief period of severe stress as a toddler, perhaps caused by a famine or an acute childhood illness. Yet his teeth did not show any evidence of the severe attrition associated with prolonged malnutrition while teeth are forming. His youth and low sugar diet must be factored into the equation, but the lack of attrition indicates that he usually had enough to eat and was probably relatively affluent. There was also evidence of occupational stresses on the warrior as he grew into a young boy. His spine revealed nodes, formed from constant pressure on the spine causing the discs to protrude; this usually occurs during childhood or adolescence, when the bones are still soft, and is evidence of hard labour activity, perhaps lifting and carrying. This was common in children in the medieval period when everyone was expected to pull their weight and started work at an early age.

The warrior's physique can reveal details of his teenage years into his early twenties. The muscles of the lower left arm were extremely well developed and there were deep muscle grooves in the upper arm, from muscles that are involved in the rotation of the forearm and flexing of the wrists and elbow. Thus, Eric was fit and healthy, probably the result of his occupation as a warrior, when upper-body agility was a necessity on both the practice and battle fields. He would, of course, have been a proficient rower, since Viking ships used oars, with or without added sail power, and rowing requires significant upper-body strength.

The bones displayed no evidence of any chronic infections or injuries that might have explained his death, but he may have died in battle or at least in a conflict situation. This can be supported by the placement of the lower right arm, clearly out of position since it was lying across the upper right arm. Some of the wrist and finger bones were partially articulated, suggesting that this occurred when the flesh (muscles and sinews) was still on the arm. While this may represent some sort of disturbance of the grave shortly after burial (also suggested for one of the other graves on the site: F598), Buckley has suggested that the lower arm may have been severed at the time of death but then simply put in with the body.

SCIENTIFIC DATA

The remains of the skeleton were scientifically dated using the radiocarbon method, a process that measures the decay of carbon-14 in the teeth. The results were somewhat surprising. Eric and two of his companions (F342 and F223) returned a much earlier date-range than anticipated, spanning the period from the late seventh to the late ninth century. Specifically, the carbon-14 determination showed that there was a 95 per cent probability that Eric died between AD670 and 880, and a 68 per cent probability that his death occurred between AD690 and 790, some fifty years before the first documented Viking settlement in Dublin. This result was matched by an identical date for one of the other warrior burials and also the warrior burial at Ship Street Great. The third warrior (F598) had a wider date-range, with a 95 per cent probability that his death occurred some time between 786 and 955, and a 68 per cent probability that it occurred between 859 and 893. While a conservative conclusion, based on the uncertainties of radio-carbon dating, might suggest a date around 841, but not after 893, for Eric's death, the statistical combination of all four graves must raise the possibility that the death of the warriors of South Great George's Street pre-dated the first recorded over-wintering in 841. Dublin, therefore, might have been a significant place of settlement and burial for the Vikings from their earliest incursions in Ireland.

Isotope analysis was also carried out on Eric's teeth in the University of Bradford and produced interesting results. This scientific test measured the oxygen isotope values, which were then compared to oxygen isotope values from tooth samples across Europe. The values differ by region, with the result that they can reveal where an individual was reared, since the composition of teeth is dictated by the groundwater they drank as children. The isotope values in Eric and one of the other warrior's teeth suggest that they spent their childhood not in Scandinavia, as one might expect, but closer to the Atlantic, perhaps somewhere in the British Isles. This warrior was evidently raised in one of the colonies in what has been termed the 'Insular Viking zone', stretching from the Faroes in the north to Ireland in the south and including the Scottish islands and the west coast of Britain.

The identification of the Insular Viking zone as Eric's place of origin ties in nicely with the shield boss found on his chest, since this has been identified as being of the Irish Sea A group, originating in this very region (see below). On the other hand, it fits less neatly with the date-range suggested by the carbon-14 dating programme. Even if Eric died in and around 841 when Dublin was established as a permanent base (and this is placing him late in the radiocarbon date-range), this suggests that he was born in the Irish Sea region in the first quarter of the ninth century. This date, in turn, is problematic for the current theories about Viking colonization in the Insular Viking zone, where there is little archaeological evidence of settlement until the mid-ninth century. The historical sources are more forthcoming. The annals record the beginning of the Viking raids along the seaboard of Ireland in the late eighth century and there are references to the taking of hostages and cattle tribute in the Dublin region in the first twenty years of the ninth century, which suggests that there were camps and settlements of some sort. This may form part of a wider picture, since Donnchadh Ó Corráin has suggested that the place-name Lothlend, which first appears in the documentary sources in the ninth century and has been thought to represent Norway, may refer to Viking Scotland and indicate that there was a Viking maritime powerbase there. It was these colonists in Scotland, then, Ó Corráin suggests, that were responsible for the second wave of more consistent and organized raids on Ireland after 820. Eric may have been one of the offspring of these earliest Viking settlers.

If the later date-range of the radiocarbon dates is applied, however, in conjunction with the isotope analysis, our warrior may have been born in Dublin and raised there, part of a large mercenary force based in the *longphort*. But this force also included true-blue Vikings, since the other two warriors returned isotope values that indicated that they were reared much farther east than Eric and, in the case of F342, probably somewhere in Scandinavia. Thus, of the four young men unearthed at this site, two came from Scandinavia, while the others were probably first-generation colonists from either Scotland or Ireland.

WHAT THE GRAVE-GOODS TELL US

One of the most exciting aspects of Eric's grave was the survival of some of his militaristic regalia, which identified him as Scandinavian and also revealed something of his social background: he was evidently a high-status individual, as is indicated by his elaborate burial. Viking shields were circular and made from wood, often painted and reinforced around the rim with leather. In general, they measure about 1m in diameter with a perforation in the centre from where the boss protruded to provide protection to the hand as it gripped the bar on the reverse. Although all the iron objects were in a poor state of preservation, the survival of the shield boss must be considered something of a lucky break, when one considers the amount of later disturbance on site (pl. 2). The iron boss, which sits on the front of the timber shield and holds it together, is perhaps the most diagnostic element of a Viking shield and this survived relatively intact, or at least enough survived to allow it to be reconstructed. It was found over the lower rib cage and vertebrae, just above the left lower arm and lying flat on the chest.

On examination, the shield was found to be a complex artefact consisting of three separate iron components – the boss that sat on the front of the timber shield, a flat iron ring (in four fragments) that held the boss to the timber shield at the back, and a cross bar (in two fragments) that may have served as a reinforcement and/or grip on the back of the shield (pl. 2). The boss was conical in shape and measured a total of 185mm, including a wide flange measuring 39mm in width. Eleven iron rivets survived at the rear or underside of the flange, which were originally hammered through the timber shield and were arranged in two rings along the outer and inner edges. The length of these rivets suggests that the actual shield board was 10mm in thickness and was composed of oak, an enduring hardwood, identified by the discovery of minute fragments of mineralized wood attached to the shaft of some of the nails and the flat iron ring. The survival of the shield boss was important from a diagnostic point of view, since different types can be provenanced to different areas of the Viking world. The conical shape of this boss was of extreme interest, as the influence for this type is now thought to be Anglo-Saxon rather than Scandinavian because the latter is usually hemispherical. The wide flange, or protruding rim, of 39mm on the boss, as opposed to the Scandinavian flange of less than 20mm, is also of interest. As a result of these features, this has been identified by Harrison as belonging to the Irish Sea Dublin Type A group. This early type can be paralleled from graves in Ormside in Cumbria, Cronk Moar in the Isle of Man and, perhaps even more closely, Millhill in Scotland. The Millhill boss has a flange of 46mm, which can be compared directly to the South Great George's Street example before conservation. Although only a small fraction survives, the Millhill example, like Eric's, also produced evidence of an iron bar at the back of the boss. The conclusion is that the boss found with 'Eric' was not Scandinavian in origin but is in the Insular tradition, the product of a craftsman operating somewhere in the Irish Sea region, perhaps even Dublin. This correlates with the isotope analysis, which matches the weapon type and the place of birth. It seems to be the case that these types of Insular weapon were in general circulation in Dublin in the ninth century and clearly available to Scandinavian-born warriors and colonists alike. Isotope analysis on another skeleton found recently in Islandbridge and excavated by Maeve Sikora showed that he was from Scandinavia but was accompanied by grave-goods that included a Dublin-type spearhead.

The corroded remains of a simple whittle-tanged iron knife were also found, lying parallel to the body but slightly under the left hip, with the blade pointing up towards his left shoulder (fig. 2.6). The position suggests that it was worn on a belt around the waist, as was a similar knife found at

Golden Lane. The knife was in relatively good condition, measuring 195mm in length with the tip of the tang (the end that is affixed to the handle) having been deliberately bent to secure the handle. This handle, although it did not survive, was evidently made of alder, since small mineralized fragments were identified at the handle end. The blade was triangular in section and had a straight back, while the cutting edge was straight with a small curve towards the tip. This was not necessarily a militaristic weapon, since knives were a vital tool for everyday life, but this was evidently a personal item.

A spread or staining of charcoal was identified along the left side of the skeleton, lying parallel at the upper arm position but diverging lower down, towards the upper legs (fig. 2.3). It was found on examination in the conservation laboratory to be a roughly rectangular piece of wood that had been completely burnt or carbonized, although not at the burial site. This was some sort of large wooden artefact or element that was burnt elsewhere and then placed partially beneath the corpse, presumably as part of the funerary ritual. Although the function of this wood is not known, another of the skeletons (F223) was also buried with a piece of burnt wood beneath the sternum and this too appeared to have been burnt elsewhere before deposition in the grave. A similar spread of fire-reddened clay was also noted at another warrior burial at Golden Lane. This was faint, but suggests that there was some

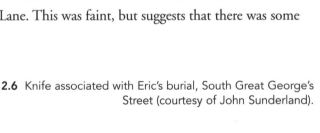

2.6 Knife associated with Eric's burial, South Great George's Street (courtesy of John Sunderland).

limited burning on site. Were these the remains of some kind of flimsy wooden coffin, which were ritually burnt before burial?

The only other item found with the warrior F196 (Eric) was a cattle horn-core, which lay directly under the body beneath the chest cavity. This was buried at the same time as Eric and therefore is likely to have been connected with the grave, much like the tusk of a wild boar buried in a warrior burial at Repton, south Derbyshire.[8] Viking grave-goods often included animal bone and, at South Great George's Street, one of the other warriors (F342) was buried with a collection of animal bones around his feet, which included dog, horse, cow, pig and sheep/goat. At Temple Bar West, another large Viking site in Dublin, the grave of a small boy aged between 7 and 11 was found just above the high-water mark of the River Liffey. It was associated with a second pit containing a bull skull, fleshed when deposited and carefully positioned with the horns facing up, surrounded by large stones. This was paralleled on the same site by a second pit, which contained seven articulated cow skulls, five with horns, placed along the edge of the pit, closely packed together and laid horizontally, but surrounding the tops of two human skulls. The exact purpose of these animal remains is unknown, but their interment and seemingly deliberate arrangement around human bodies points to a ritual of some kind, perhaps as a food source in the afterlife. Eric, with his military grave-goods, the charcoal deposit and animal bones, seems to have had a fairly elaborate funeral rite, indicating that he was of relatively high status and that he was not buried in haste.

CONCLUSION

Eric's grave, on the banks of a pool on the Poddle river, reveals a great deal of fascinating information about the men behind the earliest Viking attacks on Ireland, about whom the archaeological record to date has revealed little. This skeleton gives us a glimpse of one of the much-feared Viking predators, a man whose presence generated such terror in Ireland from the late eighth century onwards, as is graphically recorded in the documentary sources. He was probably born around the first quarter of the ninth century, if not earlier, although not in Norway as one might suspect, but rather somewhere closer to the Atlantic, perhaps in an early Viking colony in the Irish Sea region or at Dublin itself.

This warrior had survived childhood, a feat in itself, but had experienced a period of significant stress when he was between 1 and 5 years old, most likely a childhood illness or a period of severe undernourishment that was serious enough to leave an imprint on his teeth. He worked hard during his young life, as all children probably did, and he was physically very well developed at the time of his death, especially in his upper body, probably as a result of his occupation as a warrior. This man was a high-status individual, belonging to the elite of society when he died, aged between 25 and 29 years, and must have been an experienced warrior. Despite this experience and his demonstrable physical fitness, he met his end in Ireland, presumably killed at Dublin or on campaign elsewhere and brought back to the settlement at the 'black pool' that was to develop into Dyflinn. That he suffered some trauma is suggested by the fact that his right arm may have been severed, perhaps during hand-to-hand combat as a prelude to his death. After death, his community buried him with all the honours that befitted a fallen warrior of his status, which included what must have been his prized possessions – his military weapons. Viking burial was viewed as a transitional rite, a process that enabled the dead to attain peace in the next world accompanied by their personal possessions, which they would need in the afterlife. Generally, the more elaborate the grave-goods, the higher in status the individual is likely to have been. Only two grave-goods were found with the body – his knife and his shield – although he is likely to have had a sword.

The warrior's shield boss, in particular, can help flesh out details about Eric. It is very distinctive, identified by Harrison as a 'Dublin type', the conical shape and wide flange suggesting an Irish Sea influence rather than being purely Scandinavian, as does the isotope analysis. This shield may have been made in a Dublin workshop and was clearly very different from

Scandinavian shields with their hemispherical bosses. His knife, while nothing out of the ordinary, was probably the single most important tool that he possessed, since it was in everyday use, while the horn-core may have some other significance, now unknown. The large fragment of carbonized wood was also an interesting find and is probably all that survives of some sort of burning funerary rite that preceded the actual burial. This combination of interment of goods and evidence of burnt wood is not uncommon in Viking funerary rituals.

In the immediate context, Eric's grave can tell us much about what was going on in Dublin in the ninth century. He may have lived at the defended settlement on the banks of the pool, immediately east of the early Christian monastery, which is likely to have been suppressed by the newcomers. This settlement may have been the first Viking camp at Dublin, the main focus of which was the pool with its safe moorage for ships, the general expansion to the elevated ridge site to the north following slightly later. His immediate companions included not only Scandinavians born and bred, but fellow colonists as well, and this provides a window into the creation and make-up of these conglomerate armies. The early raids are thought to have been entrepreneurial initiatives, presumably under successful leaders who attracted young men eager to exploit the system of shared booty. The new data from isotopic analysis may suggest that these young men were gathered from a variety of locations and from mixed backgrounds, a reflection of the continuing close contacts between the Scandinavians by birth and the early colonists.

Finally, the discovery of Eric's grave at South Great George's Street is important in the wider context for anyone interested in the history of medieval Dublin. The identification of the cluster of graves at South Great George's Street/Ship Street/Golden Lane, in combination with the previous antiquarian 'individual graves and possible cemeteries', must now point to the presence of numerous furnished Viking burials on both sides of the river at the mouth of the Liffey, with a cluster within the Poddle valley, perhaps extending as far east as the previously known Viking cemetery at Hoggen Green. When combined with the evidence from Kilmainham and

Islandbridge in the west, this amounts to a linear spread along the Liffey valley, extending for approximately 3.7km. This astonishing number and distribution of burials must surely reflect the extraordinary numbers of young warriors who were in Dublin in the ninth century. This gives credibility to the annalistic sources that tell us how a force from their base in Dublin was capable of laying waste to the Uí Néill and the lands of the Laigin as far as Slieve Bloom in 841, the very first year of their over-wintering.[9] The archaeological evidence places Eric at that first settlement, in what must have been the centre of Viking power in Ireland at this time. Thus, even in this, the embryonic phase of Dublin's evolution, it was in effect the Viking 'capital' of Ireland.

The Slave's Tale

POUL HOLM

Sometime in the 850s a Leinsterman, Fintan, arrived in the monastery of Rheinau, near St Gallen in present-day Switzerland. He had escaped a Viking slave merchant and he came to be considered a most holy man as he decided to have himself shut up in close seclusion in a place near the northern side of the church of St Mary. He donned a hairshirt and never indulged himself at the heat of a fire or in the comfort of a bed or a bath. He devoted himself to fasts, vigils and prayers and became a wonder to the local people who came to see him, especially on the feast-day of the Irish St Brigid. When he died, probably on his recorded feast-day of 15 November 878, he had lived in this way for twenty-two years. Because of the veneration with which his monastic community remembered him, Fintan was recognized as a saint. It was probably an abbot of Rheinau who commissioned a biography of Fintan, *Vita Sancti Findani*, and a tenth- or eleventh-century version of it survives to tell his story.[1]

Fintan had lived for five years as a novice and monk before he decided to seclude himself and we may therefore assume that he arrived at Rheinau around 851. On arrival he declared himself to be 51 years of age, already an old man, and so would have been born around 800. Irishmen were well known to monastic establishments at the time, as many before had brought the holy word to the Continent. Fintan made himself well known from the start by beginning a strict practice of fast. During those early years he must have shared the story of his troubled past with his brethren.

These troubles began in Ireland, his homeland, where he was twice taken captive by Vikings. The first time, he had been sent by his father to approach a marauding party of Northmen who had taken his sister and many other women captive. He brought with him a ransom, probably in the form of brooches and other silver, some followers and an interpreter, presumably one who spoke both Irish and Norse. The Vikings seized Fintan, put him in chains and brought him to their ships. He remained there for two days until the Vikings decided that it was in their interest to take the ransom, ensuring that such an exchange might happen again. The danger remained, however, since Fintan told his scribe that on a subsequent occasion the same enemies pursued him and he fled into a house and hid behind a 'door'. Strangely, the Vikings were unable to find him, although they were running to and fro in their search. Perhaps Fintan was able to escape from his pursuers by taking refuge not behind the door of the house, but in a souterrain or some other concealed place.[2]

His third encounter with the Vikings did not go so well. While the previous events seem to have come out of the blue, in typical Viking hit-and-run style, the circumstances this time were much more complicated. Events were set in motion when Fintan's father killed an opponent. The victim's chieftain came to avenge the slaughter and set the house on fire, killing Fintan's father after he had escaped from the burning building. Fintan and his brother were in another house, which was put on fire as well. His brother was killed, but Fintan fought his way out. The two sides eventually made peace and compensation was paid to Fintan's side. This peace was a clever trick, however. Fintan was invited to a feast and, when he sat in the middle of his enemies, a band of Vikings entered and seized him. His Irish enemies had contracted with the Norse to bring him to their ships at the nearby coast.

In the next weeks or months Fintan was a commodity sold off first by his captors to another party, then another, until finally he ended up in the hands of a ship's crew that intended to head home, presumably to Scandinavia, with a number of captives. The journey went north along the Scottish Isles and somewhere en route they encountered additional Norse ships. When the crews exchanged visits, one of Fintan's captors saw that a member of the other crew was the man who had killed his brother and immediately cut him down. As battle broke out between the two crews,

Fintan tried to be of assistance to his side, even as he was in chains. The other ships' crews eventually calmed the fight and Fintan's vessel continued northwards. In recognition of Fintan's loyalty during the fight, he was released from his chains.

Soon after, they arrived in the Orkney Islands, close to the land of the Picts. According to the *Vita*, Fintan was allowed to walk free on the island and seized the opportunity to hide in a rock cave by the sea. When the tide came in, he was concealed on all sides from his captors who were searching for him above. His enemies left the following day and Fintan marshalled his strength. On the third day he plunged into the water and miraculously made his way to the mainland. The *Vita* claims that his clothes became rigid so that he could not sink. Eventually he met kind people who took him to the bishop, who had been trained in Ireland and knew the language. Fintan stayed with him for two years before he decided to visit holy shrines on the Continent. He travelled all the way to Rome on foot and spent another four years as a priest in the service of an Alamannian aristocrat before his final journey to Rheinau. We may assume therefore that his last Viking encounter took place some time around 840.

Fintan's life was exceptional and it is the only story we have as told by an Irish slave. We have no way, of course, to corroborate the details. As it is, the story fits what we know about Viking and Irish encounters in the ninth century. Fintan's first encounter with the Northmen was occasioned by their abduction of a number of females and a parallel is in the Irish annals for the year 821 when 'they carried off a great number of women into captivity' from Howth. We know that Vikings often preferred to take women and children with them, as they were more easily subdued. Genetics have confirmed literary evidence that the first settlers in Iceland were Norwegian men and an ethnic mix of females, many of whom were of Irish descent.[3] The freeing of captives in return for a ransom was a regular occurrence and the collusion between Fintan's enemies and the Vikings was nothing unusual either. The annals tell of repeated alliances between Irish and Vikings from the 850s onwards and it is highly likely that earlier instances such as this may have occurred.[4] Indeed, some of the Irish copied

Viking tactics. In 847 the Annals of Ulster tell that an island in the Shannon was occupied by a great band of 'sons of death' of the Luighne and Gailenga 'who had been plundering the territories after the manner of the heathens'.[5]

Viking slave raids are well documented both in English and in Frankish annals. Between 834 and 896 we hear of twenty-six attacks when captives were taken and in a couple of instances it is stated expressly that the captives were sold as slaves (fig. 3.1). The Anglo-Saxon Chronicle mentions the taking of captives in 921 and 1011 and opponents of the Danes were sold on the market in 1036.[6] Many slave raids will of course have gone unreported both in western and in eastern Europe. We do not know which areas were hit hardest, but because of the exceptionally good documentation afforded by the Irish annals there is no doubt that Ireland took its fair share. Between the years 800 and 1100 we hear of about six hundred clashes between Norse and Irish combatants. Of these, 320 were attacks on monastic settlements and the rest were secular engagements. Most of the entries leave us in the dark regarding the casualties, but nineteen entries explicitly mention the taking of captives and in another eleven cases we learn of the ransoming of eminent prisoners; the fate of the rest is a matter of conjecture. We cannot know how many were taken prisoner in these attacks but some entries do leave us with an impression of substantial numbers. A thousand people were taken from Armagh in 869 and 'a great prey of Angles and Britons and Picts' were brought in captivity to Dublin in 871.

We know that chains were used by the Norse to keep their captives from escaping (fig. 3.2). A find from the Viking *longphort* of Linn Duachaill reveals that slaves might be chained together to prevent their escape. Similar chains are known from non-Viking contexts in Ireland, indicating that the Irish would have used them to restrain captives in their own battles.[7] Another way of preventing flight would be to bring captives to an island. According to the Annals of the Four Masters, Dalkey Island was used for this purpose, since one unfortunate abbot who had not been ransomed drowned in 939 attempting to flee from his prison. One way of securing one's property might of course be to leave a permanent mark on the captive's body. A Danish twelfth-century law states that 'if it happens that

3.1 Tablet depicting slaves from Inchmarnock, Firth of Clyde, Scotland (photograph by Chris Lowe, Headland Archaeology, Creative Commons Attribution 3.0).

someone takes a free man and cuts up one nostril, then he pays a quarter wergild [the value of a human life]. But if he cuts up both nostrils, he pays half wergild. Because it is the mark of a slave and not of a free man'.[8] Cutting up the nostrils would have been an effective way of marking one's property but hardly conducive to getting a good price on the market; accordingly this measure was presumably taken only once the owner had decided to keep the slave permanently.

As a male, perhaps by then in his forties, Fintan was probably lucky not to be killed but brought away as a slave. If he had not escaped, his future would have been totally dependent on the whim of his master. Because he seems to have won his master's favour, he might have hoped to become a trusted servant rather than a lowly agricultural worker. Some slaves did

3.2 Slave chain from near Strokestown, Co. Roscommon
(by permission of the National Museum of Ireland; reg. no. Wk29).

succeed in making it to a recognized position in their new country, such as Tóki Smith, whom we know from the runic stone that he raised in memory of Þorgísl Guðmundr's son. Þorgísl was Tóki's master who gave him freedom and gold, or maybe even kinship – the Danish word is ambiguous. Tóki is a Danish name but he may have been a foreigner since we know that slave owners were in the habit of giving their slaves new names. According to the Icelandic Book of Settlement or *Landnámabók*, a certain Ketill, for example, brought six Irish slaves to his farm in Iceland and they were all given Norse names, Þórmóðr, Flóki, Kóri, Svartr and two called Skorri. Others were allowed to keep their names, rendered in Norse as Kormakr, Dufan (?), Dufþakr (Dubhthach), Kjaran, Melkofr and Njál.[9]

An example of the naming of slaves is preserved in the Icelandic Song of Ríg, or *Rígsþula*. The poem probably grew out of a folktale about the origin of the three social estates – slaves, freemen and nobles – and tells how the

Norse god Heimdallr had offspring with three women. The oldest gave birth to ugly, swarthy children, Þræll (slave) and Þir, who beget children themselves. They are destined to become slaves and are given names such as Fjosnir ('cattle-man'), Hreim ('shouter') and Kleggi ('horse-fly'), Kefsir ('concubine keeper') and Fulnir ('stinker'). The offspring of the two other women are destined to become freeborn peasants and noblemen, and of the latter eventually the finest of them all is born, Rígr Konungr. His name betrays an Irish connection, *ríg* being the Irish for 'king', and his name is the finest double-barrel of all names, as *konungr* means 'king' in Old Norse. The poem clearly draws on the close and problematic contacts between the Norse and the Irish.[10]

A harsh end awaited a few captives in Scandinavia. Thietmar of Merseburg reports that every ninth year in January the heathens of Lejre, a royal seat in Denmark, would sacrifice ninety-nine humans, dogs, horses and cocks. A similar gory story is told of Swedish Uppsala where, according to Adam of Bremen, every ninth year nine males of every species would be sacrificed and hung in the sacred wood. Thietmar may have improved on the story by multiplying by ten and indeed the stories may not be true at all. Nevertheless, there is ample archaeological evidence that slaves occasionally would be sacrificed upon the death of their master or mistress. Ibn Fadlan, an Arab traveller who reported on the Vikings in Russia, claims that the servants would volunteer to follow in death, but archaeology makes clear that not all went freely, since some victims had their hands and feet tied before the sacrifice (fig. 3.3).[11]

Most slaves were probably destined for hard agricultural labour. The twelfth-century Norwegian Frostathing Law states that a full peasant farm at the time would have twelve cows, two horses and three slaves. We cannot know whether this was indeed an average complement of a Norwegian farm – but assuming so the total number of slaves in Norway at the time would have been in the order of 50,000–75,000.[12] Many, if not most of them, would have been of Irish descent. The total number of settlers in Iceland in the tenth century is estimated at around 20,000 and it does not seem unreasonable to suggest that 4,000–5,000 would have been slaves,

3.3 Stone image depicting human sacrifice from Stora Hammars, Gotland (courtesy of Anders Andrén).

almost all of them of Celtic origin. Some Irish slaves are likely to have been brought to the Norse settlements in the Hebrides, Shetland, Orkney and the Faroes. As late as the early twentieth century, a black-haired person would be called *traelfangin* ('slave-taken') on the local dialect in the island of Fetlar, clearly an indication of fair-haired Norse perceptions of the Gaels.[13] Denmark had a much larger population than Norway and a rich slave market at Hedeby, feeding off both western and eastern supplies. Sweden might also be a destination for an Irish slave, as indeed we are told in both *Landnámabók* and *Laxdœla saga* of Melkorka, an Irish princess who was sold on the slave market of Brenneyar off present-day Gothenburg by a Russian merchant to a would-be Icelandic settler.

It is likely that the slave trade of the Vikings developed from the haphazard conditions described in the *Vita Findani* to a larger and much more regular market in the tenth and eleventh centuries and Irish slaves may have been sold off to many other places. King Canute's sister is said to have been a capable slave merchant, buying up people in England and sending them to Denmark, 'especially girls, whose beauty and age rendered them more valuable, that she might accumulate money by this horrid traffic', as a slightly later report tells us.[14] Other likely destinations were the courts of Normandy and the Spanish Caliphate. We know that there was a flow of humans, particularly from the Slavic borders of the Continent into Muslim Spain, but we have no way of knowing how many Irish went that long route. Once captured, a slave could be sold many times and while Christian rulers in principle abhorred the slave trade, they left it mainly to

Jewish merchants to service the transportation of people across the Alps to the slave market of Venice or from Verdun down the Rhône to Spain. In the tenth century Verdun was a regular 'factory' of eunuchs for the court of Córdoba, while Venice serviced the palaces of the Levant.[15]

We have one cruel contemporary comment on the fate of being sold into unknown territories. It comes to us through a poem of the first quarter of the eleventh century by a Norman, Warner of Rouen. He ridicules an Irish poet, Moriuht, evidently his competitor for courtly favour. Moriuht is described as an ugly, swarthy character whose wife Glicerium has been captured by Vikings. Moriuht's search takes him through England and Saxony until he finds her and her daughter living as slaves in Rouen. Warner intimates that Moriuht succeeds in freeing them only by debasing himself sexually. The poem is devoid of any moral outrage against slavery and clearly uses the stigma of serfdom, not least the loss of sexual control, to vilify the Irishman.[16]

One of the largest slave markets in Ireland was in Dublin, which by the tenth century was a major port town with extensive trade relations. Not all slaves were sold off to foreign markets since the Hiberno-Norse needed servants, concubines and labourers for themselves. We know only the name of one of them, Kolbein, a Norse name. He made his way into the annals in 989 when he killed Iron-knee, king of Dublin, in a drunken fight. We do not know how many people lived in Dublin and still less how many slaves there would have been. I have made a claim that the town and its surroundings may well have had a Norse population of around 10,000.[17] If we go by the proportionalities assumed above for Norway and Iceland, this would indicate a couple of thousand slaves, but this is pure conjecture.

What we do know is that after the Battle of Tara in 980, the king of Meath is reputed to have freed all the Irish slaves of Dublin. The *Chronicum Scotorum* reports that Máel Sechnaill proclaimed 'let every one of the Irish who is in the territory of the foreigners in servitude and bondage depart thence to his own territory with peace and happiness'. In 999 Brian Bóruma and Máel Sechnaill did the same after the victory over Leinster and the mercenaries of Dublin, indicating that slavery continued despite the original proclamation in 980. These were difficult times for Dublin and no less so for the other Viking settlements, some of which succumbed to Irish overlordship at the time.

The inhabitants of Dublin itself continued slave raids when possible and could not always be trusted by their Irish allies. In 1023 the king of Brega attended an assembly of the Dublin Thing (the legal assembly of the town) to negotiate with the Norse under the assumption that he was granted protection. Nevertheless, he was held captive, 'taken overseas' and 'carried to the east', as the Annals of Ulster and the Annals of Tigernach tell us. While the Vikings occasionally were able to lead major attacks and secure slaves for its market, it is doubtful whether the town would have been as rich as it clearly was, judging by the abundance of eleventh-century archaeological finds, if it had not had other sources of trade than its own pillage. By this time, however, the Vikings were not the only slave raiders.

Slavery was widespread in Ireland even before the arrival of the Vikings. The most common names for slaves in Irish were *mug* for male and *cumal* for female. *Cumal* was also widely used as a unit of value for cattle and land. There were several ways of becoming a slave. You might be taken as a prisoner of war, you might offer yourself or your children as payment if you incurred a heavy debt or you could be born of slaves. Medieval Irish sources for slavery are abundant but impressionistic. Ship raids on Britain in the fifth century after the collapse of the Roman Empire provided prisoners of war who became slaves.[18] These raids seem to have ceased as a result of the stabilization of Britain in the seventh century. Martyrologies often refer to slave labour as an image of personal debasement. The *vita* of St Senan tells of the men of Corcu Baiscind who were admonished to obey St Senan in order not to suffer such hunger that 'a man would sell his son and daughter in distant territories for nourishment'. A *vita* of the ninth century relates that one of the tasks St Ciarán had to perform as a slave was grinding grain every day. Slaves are never associated with husbandry but mainly with heavy agricultural labour such as sowing, harrowing, threshing and grinding.

The impact of the Viking attacks and subsequent settlements was to accentuate slavery as a social institution among the Irish. Viking warfare did not respect the sanctity of monasteries and brought about a change in the norms of warfare. This included an acceptance of reducing prisoners of war to slave status. Just as the 'sons of death' had emulated the Vikings, the practice of slave raids increasingly took hold among the Irish. We know of forty-one instances of the Irish taking captives rather than just hostages between 913 and 1149. We hear of 200, 300 and even 1,200 people being taken captive in a single raid. It is likely that such large numbers ensured that some captives were ransomed or sold off to other buyers. In 942 the prisoners are said to have been women, children and non-combatant men, while the warriors were killed. In 1089 the Uí Briúin Bréifne were attacked and several of them taken captive, while their own prisoners, who were kept on an island in Lough Oughter, were freed. In revenge, the Uí Briúin attacked the churches of their opponents and led many prisoners away.

The major struggles for the high-kingship of Ireland before 1014 and again in the years leading up to 1116 greatly increased the taking of captives. The Cenél nEógain king Flaithbertach was the leading slaver in a number of actions on neighbouring territories. In 1011 he united with the son of Brian Bóruma and allegedly took many cows and 300 *brait* ('captives'), a word hitherto restricted to Viking assaults, from the Cenél Conaill. The Annals of Ulster record that he plundered the Ulaid in the following year and 'took the greatest spoils, both in captives and cattle that a king ever took, though they are not counted'. In later years, the annals repeatedly note the taking of large numbers of prisoners. The rising power of the northern over-kings is marked in the annals by heavy exactions on neighbouring kingdoms. Likewise, the Ua Conchobair kings of Connacht, who were close at times to achieving total supremacy over Ireland, practised this new kind of warfare in their campaigns. The climax came in 1109 when Muirchertach of the Dál Cais mustered a large force against the Uí Briúin of Connacht and took many captives from the islands of Loch Oughter. The Uí Briúin took revenge upon Meath, which was allied to Muirchertach, by burning and killing and leading off many captives. The final blows to Dál Cais supremacy were accompanied by great predatory expeditions in 1115 and 1116, but the prisoners of the last campaign were afterwards released in homage to God and to St Flannán of Killaloe – the patron saint of the Dál Cais.

What were the driving motives behind the taking of large numbers of prisoners by Irish kings of the eleventh and early twelfth centuries? First, there was a striking similarity between the warfare of the Norse rulers of Dublin and Irish kings. From the Vikings, the Irish learnt simple lessons such as how to humiliate kings by imprisoning large numbers of their subjects and they put this tactic to their own use. Furthermore, Irish cattle raids and petty warfare between minor kings took on a larger and more devastating character when the Irish invited Viking warriors into their wars of conquest and paid them in kind with the wealth of the enemy, including prisoners of war. There was a ready slave market for these victims of Irish battles in Dublin and other Hiberno-Norse towns.

We know that the great struggles of the over-kings for supremacy were to a large degree decided by the use of naval fleets. These fleets were either indirectly controlled by the over-king as a consequence of their control of Norse towns or they were hired from Norse settlements in Ireland or the Scottish Isles. The Dublin fleet was certainly available in return for the payment of slaves and cattle. In the second half of the eleventh century Gruffydd ap Cynan built up his power in Wales with the help of the Norse fleet and paid repeatedly in slaves. Slave raiding was condoned and perpetrated by up-and-coming Irish high-kings, as is evidenced in the cases of Leinster, Cenél nEógain and Ua Conchobair kings. Dublin's slave market was thriving from this trade well into the twelfth century, despite the town being under Irish rule.

We have much circumstantial evidence of the importance of slavery to Irish kings in early twelfth-century writings such as *Lebor na cert* (Book of rights) and *Cogadh Gáedhel re Gallaibh* (The war of the Gaedhel with the Gall). The distinction in these texts between male and female slaves reveals some functions of slavery. Female slaves are referred to as 'full-grown', 'swarthy', 'fair', 'graceful' and 'valuable' and the king of Leinster was obliged to give 'eight women whom he has not dishonoured'. Male slaves are described as 'lads', 'hard-working', 'strong-fisted', 'willing', 'expensive' and 'spirited'. If we may deduce anything from these descriptions, the slaves seem primarily to have been intended for the household, as servants and concubines. The old use of *cumal* for a female slave was evidently obsolete by 1100 and instead *mná* (*daera*) ('servile woman') or the linguistically crude *banmog* (literally translated as 'woman-slave') were used. Further, *Lebor na cert* draws a clear distinction between native and foreign slaves ('foreigners who do not know Irish', 'women from over the great sea'), an indication not only that slaves were recruited by internal warfare but also that some were supplied by foreign trade.

In the eleventh century, Dublin furnished slave traders in the British Isles (Anglo-Saxon as well as Norse), Scandinavia and Iceland. In 1102, however, the Normans prohibited the slave trade in England on religious grounds, while traders became increasingly despised. Demand in Scandinavia declined for the same religious and social reasons as in Britain. The Irish slave raids and slave trade seem therefore to have petered out in the twelfth century. Slavery as such did not end overnight and indeed the Irish synod of 1170 welcomed the Anglo-Norman conquest as just punishment for the abuses of the slave trade. As late as 1235, the mark of slavery was still felt by some people; in Waterford in this same year there was a man known as Philippus Leysing, Philip the manumitted, or freed slave. Tens of thousands of slaves' tales could be told if the sources survived. We are lucky to have one – the *Vita Sancti Findani*.

The Mother's Tale

HOWARD B. CLARKE

Before turning to Gormlaith herself, a number of general considerations should be stated, starting with the obvious point that she lived a long time ago. She died in the year 1030, as three contemporary sets of annals record, that is to say, about forty generations from our own time. We have only to consider what life was like for the majority of Irish people only six or seven generations ago – before, during and immediately after the Great Famine – to realize how different the past can be. Readers will also instinctively understand that life for members of social elites was fundamentally different from that of the vast underclass. The same was true a thousand years ago, in Gormlaith's lifetime.

One of those fundamental differences that affected everyone living then was low population. We have no figures of the kind provided by modern censuses, but my own (published) guestimate for the island of Ireland c.1000 is half a million.[1] Dublin itself, an emerging Viking town in Gormlaith's youth, would have had about 3,500 to 4,000 inhabitants – men, women and children.[2] Life in those circumstances was unavoidably more intimate; people would have known, or known of, one another much more readily than we do. As the archaeology of Viking Dublin has shown so vividly, the mass of the people, including slaves, lived cheek-by-jowl in close proximity to their neighbours. Nothing like a royal hall has yet been found archaeologically, but the ruling family descended from Ívarr inn Beinlausi (the Boneless, d. 873) presumably lived in a compound inside the defences, perhaps on the site of the later castle, overlooking the pool of Dublin that sheltered the all-important fleet of ships. At the time of her first marriage and still in her mid-teens c.970, Gormlaith would have been a familiar figure as she rode through the streets of Dyflinn. In those days, celebrity arose from social status and from genuine force of personality, rather than being artificially media-driven as it now tends to be.

A second general factor is low life expectancy. Again we have no figures, but when statistically valid information starts to become available, in thirteenth-century England (before the Black Death), average life expectancy appears to have been in the low thirties.[3] A woman like Gormlaith, born say in the mid-950s, would not have expected to live into her seventies. Death in childbirth remained common for centuries; its sharp reduction in comparatively recent times is one of the main reasons for dramatic population growth worldwide. Psychologically, therefore, young people still in their teens – boys and girls – would have been attuned to the idea of getting on with life in all its aspects; not a lot more of it was in prospect, statistically speaking.

Coupled with this was another important facet of life – the sexualization of most boys and girls at a very early age. Nowadays we may deplore this, but Gormlaith and her contemporaries would not have thought in such terms. One reason had nothing to do with morality; it had to do with the practical circumstances of life for most people. The archaeology of Viking Age Dublin has revealed conclusively that the standard dwelling house – Patrick Wallace's Type 1 – comprised only one room with a central hearth, side 'aisles' for seating and sleeping, and corner compartments used for a variety of purposes.[4] A central fact of life would have been that all of the occupants – whether husband, wife and children, adult siblings of those parents, grandparents if they happened to survive that long, and even domestic slaves – all lived and slept in that single space, unless a smaller Type 2 house stood in the back yard. There was little or no privacy for anyone. In later centuries it sometimes became customary for the husband and wife to occupy the middle of the bed, or bedding area, male children sleeping on their father's side and female ones on their mother's. Even so, parental intercourse must have taken place from time to time. In such circumstances young children not only knew the facts of life; they saw them in operation at close quarters as a matter of course. Childhood experience of sexual activity on the part of adults may have been one motive behind its large-scale avoidance in the Middle Ages by entering a monastery or nunnery in later life.

Ironically the chief exceptions may have been children brought up, by parents or foster-parents, in aristocratic households, whose halls may have contained screens that provided some measure of privacy in daytime and at night-time. Even so, there were other social factors that would have led to early sexualization, as I shall mention later. A standard feature of such households, especially royal ones, was early politicization. The political world in which Gormlaith grew up in the mid-tenth century was extremely complicated. Ireland was a world of multiple kingship, with the major provincial dynasties continually vying with one another, coincidentally with a multiplicity of petty kingdoms inside the provincial ones.[5] Political life in Leinster in Gormlaith's day was peculiarly intricate at the level of the provincial kingship itself. She belonged to the Uí Fáeláin sept, based at Naas, which shared the provincial kingship with two other Uí Dúnlainge septs – Uí Dúnchada based at Newcastle Lyons and Uí Muiredaig based at Mullaghmast, near Athy. The kingship appears to have been shared on a roughly rotational basis. If she was born *c.*955, the king of Leinster was Tuathal of Uí Muiredaig (947–58); rulership then passed to Cellach of Uí Dúnchada (958–66) and after that to her own Uí Fáeláin father, Murchad mac Finn (966–72). The cycle was then repeated: Augaire of Uí Muiredaig (972–8) and Domnall Cláen and his son Donnchad of Uí Dúnchada (978–1003 in succession), before her own brother Máel Mórda was installed, by her ex-husband Brian Bóruma, in 1003.[6] Meanwhile, up the road from Naas, there was a very special kingdom, that of the Vikings of Dublin. The possibilities for political machinations were endless, both for kings and would-be kings, as well as for royal daughters and wives with a taste for intrigue and opportunism.

Political gamesmanship (and gameswomanship) was controlled to some degree by constraints of a legal nature. In Ireland at this time there were two types of legal authority, one much more forceful than the other. The more forceful was customary law, inherited from the past and set down in writing in remarkable detail as early as the seventh century AD. Our sources take the form of law-tracts dating from that time and a whole series of subsequent writings. The force of customary law in Gormlaith's day was not necessarily the same as it had been back in the seventh century, but the impression one gets is that traditional law remained dominant *c.*1000 and indeed for long afterwards in Gaelic Ireland. The legal status of women was similar in many ways to that in other patriarchal societies. At the social level of a typical farmer, his wife was expected to bear and to rear children, to mind the hearth and home, and to partake in certain tasks related to domestic animals such as butter-making. Practical skills associated with the making and mending of clothing were assumed as standard. Thus, in Anglo-Saxon England a typical *húsbonda*, 'householder' (hence husband) would have had a pliant *wifmann*, 'weaving person', 'woman' (hence wife). As in England, however, the lifestyle of high-status Irish women was presumably different. The legal texts have a lot to say about marital arrangements of such women.

Women had no independent legal capacity. As young girls they were subject to the authority of their father; as married women to that of their husband; and as widows to that of a son or, failing that, a brother or other senior male relative. Most women got married at least once and they married young, commonly in their teens. Indeed, later on in the Middle Ages, the legal age of marriage in feudal society was settled at fourteen for a boy and twelve for a girl. At the level of kingship, medieval politics was dominated by two principal concerns: the acquisition and retention of power and influence, and the acquisition and retention of landed property and movable wealth. In order to achieve those ends, one avenue was the marriage market and, to exploit that market to maximum effect, two vital social mechanisms were prevalent. One was serial marriage, for both men and women. Three or four marriages in a single lifetime, short as it often was, were commonplace, the maximum recorded for both sexes in Ireland being six (as compared with Charlemagne's nine!).

The other social mechanism was more complicated in its management by the husband. This was polygyny, a form of polygamy in which a man had a chief, official wife and one, or sometimes more than one, secondary wife or concubine.[7] Apart from mere sexual gratification, there was an entirely practical justification for polygyny: the first wife might not produce a son at all, or one who survived into adulthood. From a king's point of view, male succession was crucial, hence the widespread practice and indeed social acceptance of polygyny. In this, Ireland was in no way unique, for polygyny was normal in Anglo-Saxon and Frankish royal lineages. Accordingly, the Irish lawyers obligingly provided rules for most eventualities: for example, one text permits the chief wife to inflict any non-fatal injury on the second wife for a period of three days (presumably after her husband's second marriage), whereas in retaliation the second wife can only scratch, pull hair, speak abusively or inflict other minor injuries.[8]

There was one other mechanism that had multiple political and social consequences and that was entitlement to divorce, on the part of both husbands and wives. High-status Irishmen appear to have divorced their wives more or less at will, but wives were accorded at least a dozen grounds in customary law for divorcing their husbands. These included the predictable ones, such as being sterile, impotent or homosexual, or becoming a monk or a priest. Other grounds were subtler: blabbing about what went on, or did not go on, in the marriage bed (regarded as breach of privacy), or becoming so fat as to make sexual intercourse physically impossible. Wife-beating was permitted provided that no visible blemishes or scars resulted, in which case a wife could sue for divorce.[9]

These were some of the secular legal constraints in Gormlaith's world. The other set was embedded in canon law, which of course discouraged current social norms such as serial marriage, polygyny and divorce. To all appearances, it failed both in Gormlaith's lifetime and for many centuries to come, at least in Gaelic Ireland and in the upper social circles thereof.[10] Gormlaith's socio-political world would have moulded her as it did most women of her class. How, then, should we judge her?

One sure sign of Gormlaith's social status is quite simply her name. The first element *gorm* has a primary meaning of 'blue', but also a range of other meanings such as 'illustrious' and 'splendid'. The second element *flaith* means 'domain', 'kingdom', 'principality' and the more abstract 'sovereignty'.[11] In other words, her name had strong aristocratic connotations and was borne by other high-status women in early medieval Ireland. Whether the daughters of mere farmers were ever dignified by such a name we do not know (nowadays, of course, anyone can be called Órlaith). Our Gormlaith was born, if not in the purple, at least in a richly blue hue. As I have already indicated, her father Murchad was the provincial king from 966 to 972, until he was killed treacherously by his Uí Dúnchada rival, Domnall Cláen, while her brother Máel Mórda ruled over the province from 1003 to 1014. At those times her family would have collected (or tried to collect) tributary payments from all of the petty kingdoms of Leinster. Naas, surrounded by the fertile farmland of the Liffey plain and situated not far from the kingdom's most prestigious church, at Kildare, would have been a centre of prestige and wealth.

The dates of Gormlaith's marriages are not recorded. Her first was certainly to the king of Dublin, Óláfr Sigtryggsson, nicknamed Kváran, 'sandal'. A likely and chronologically possible date would have been in the late 960s, after her father Murchad had become the king of Leinster. She was his second wife and he was probably at least thirty years her senior. Óláfr was having trouble with the reigning high-king, his former brother-in-law Domnall ua Néill, and in those circumstances he may have been seeking a powerful and not-too-distant political ally. Part of the deal could have been that Dubliners were exempted from paying tribute to the provincial king. Culturally it was a mixed marriage, a Norse-speaking and allegedly apostate Scandinavian matched with an Irish-speaking and presumably Christian Irish woman. There are hints that Óláfr knew Irish and it is possible that Gormlaith went to the trouble of learning Old Norse, or was even obliged to do so. The language or languages of the marriage bed are unknown, though her husband in Irish sources becomes Amlaíb (cf. McAuliffe), suggestive perhaps of mutual bilingualism. Nor do we know whether this marriage lasted for its natural course, until Óláfr, having suffered a major military defeat at the Battle of Tara in 980, retired as a penitent to the monastic island of Iona off the western coast of Scotland.[12] At any rate by 980 Gormlaith was an abandoned wife and by the following year a widow. By any standard, even canonical, she was free to remarry and, of course, any ambitious young man could in his turn seek her hand in marriage.

Gormlaith's possible second marriage is not recorded or even hinted at in any source that can be regarded as contemporary. Nor is this marriage alluded to in the text known as the Banshenchas.[13] Rather it occurs first in a quatrain embedded in mid-twelfth-century genealogical material in the Book of Leinster.[14] This was borrowed much later by the Four Masters in the 1630s and added to her death-notice.[15] Here is what it says in the twelfth-century version:

> Three buck leaps (*trí lémmend*) were made by Gormlaith
> Which no other woman shall do until Doomsday:
> A buck-leap into Dublin, a leap into Tara,
> A leap into Cashel, the plain of mounds above all.[16]

In Modern Irish the word for a leap is *léim* and in Old and Middle Irish contexts it is associated with fish and with horses, with connotations of rapid or precipitate motion. In this human context, there is a modern English parallel in the idea of leaping into someone's bed, whether one's own or that of another man or woman. Clearly our mid-twelfth-century author disapproved of Gormlaith's actions, but this is only to be expected of an age of church reform, notwithstanding its general lack of success in many social spheres. Donegal-based Franciscans in the age of the Counter-Reformation would naturally have been equally disapproving. Their death-notice for Gormlaith also includes a piece of demonstrable misinformation, not in the original, to the effect that she bore for her second husband, Máel Sechnaill mac Domnaill of Mide, a son called Conchobar.[17] In reality Conchobar was Máel Sechnaill's grandson (and a son of the abbot of Clonard), who became the Clann Cholmáin king of Mide in 1030 (the year of Gormlaith's death) and ruled until 1073.[18]

An association between Gormlaith and Conchobar's grandfather may have had some connection with events that took place in 989. At the start

4.1 Silver penny of Sitric Silkenbeard (© Trustees of the British Museum).

of that year the king of Dublin was Járnkné Óláfsson (gaelicized as Glúniarainn mac Amlaíb), who was murdered by his own slave, Colbain (Norse Kolbein), while drunk, pinpointing one of the often overlooked realities of socio-economic life in the town.[19] As the relatively new and forceful high-king, Máel Sechnaill mac Domnaill intervened.[20] He led his army to Dublin and won a battle fought somewhere outside the fortified main settlement. He and his men then set siege to the latter for nearly three weeks, making the defenders surrender for lack of fresh water. The punishment was sophisticated if not very practical: the householders were obligated to pay a tax of one ounce of gold each Christmas night, 'for ever' as *Chronicum Scotorum* says.[21] A new king of Dublin had to be chosen. In 989 three of Óláfr's known sons were still living – Haraldr (Aralt), Dubgall and Sigtryggr (Sitric 'Silkenbeard'). It was the latter, Gormlaith's son, who was elevated and there can be little doubt that Máel Sechnaill was the kingmaker (fig. 4.1). Though we cannot be certain, the other sons were probably the children of Óláfr's first wife, in which case Gormlaith's son was given preference over them. One explanation may be that she and Máel Sechnaill were then married to, or otherwise associated with, one another, or at least had been in the past. (These events, by the way, were employed by the city authorities to justify Dublin's pseudo-millennium back in 1988!)

One of the great historical themes of the 990s in Ireland is the intense political rivalry that developed between Máel Sechnaill and that better-known southern upstart, Brian Bóruma. By 997 they had agreed to carve up the island between them as two hegemonies, Máel Sechnaill keeping the northern half and Brian taking the southern half, including crucially the kingdom of Dublin. Wife-swapping may not be an altogether modern phenomenon: at any rate, Gormlaith took up with, or was taken up by, Brian, becoming his second wife. She was still young enough to bear him a son, Donnchad, who would in due course become his successor as king of Munster. A Munster takeover of the whole of Leinster was not welcome, as Gormlaith presumably discovered. Her relationship with Brian was probably fairly short-lived, for by 997 he had taken another woman as his third wife.[22] Rebellion was in the air, starting in Dublin and conceivably spurred on by a rejected Gormlaith. On the penultimate day of the year 999 the Dubliners fought and lost the Battle of Glenn Máma, perhaps near Newcastle Lyons, with an expeditionary force led by Brian. Haraldr was killed, Sigtryggr expelled and the town burnt to the ground.[23]

As always on such occasions, a political settlement was reached, though with fairly extraordinary terms. Sigtryggr was restored as king of Dublin and was provided with a new wife, Sláine, a daughter of Brian Bóruma by his first marriage. Accordingly Gormlaith's son by her first marriage was married to a step-daughter born to the first wife (Echrad) of her third, though former, husband. In 1003 Brian, now high-king himself in succession to Máel Sechnaill, deposed the Uí Dúnchada king of Leinster, Donnchad (984–1003), and replaced him with Gormlaith's (Uí Fáeláin) brother, Máel Mórda. Was this done at the request of, even out of respect for, his own ex-wife, whose son, Sigtryggr, was now his recently acquired son-in-law? Conceivably so, for Donnchad's father was the man who had treacherously murdered the father of Gormlaith and Máel Mórda back in 972.

The political settlement of both kingdoms, Dublin and Leinster, in the opening years of the new millennium brought stability for ten years. But relations soured again in 1013 and the dramatic outcome was the climactic battle fought at Clontarf in the following spring. The machinations leading up to that event are the context for the other dimension of Gormlaith's reputation – that of a wicked queen stirring up hatred of her ex-husband

and inciting either her brother Máel Mórda to rebel against his overlord Brian or her son Sigtryggr to kill Brian. The two sources for this characterization are literary and considerably later. One is the Munster propaganda text *Cogadh Gáedhel re Gallaibh* composed in the time of Muirchertach Ua Briain, Brian Bóruma's great-grandson, in the early twelfth century. This is the basis of most of the myths and misimpressions associated with the great battle. The other source is part of a lost saga, putatively called *Brjáns saga*, embedded towards the close of one of the best-known Icelandic family sagas, *Brennu-Njáls saga* ('burnt' Njál referring to his fate of being deliberately burnt alive by his enemies in his own house, a real-life occurrence in medieval Iceland). Whereas the scene is set at Kincora in *Cogadh Gáedhel re Gallaibh*, Dublin is the implied location in *Brennu-Njáls saga*. The details surrounding the role attributed to Gormlaith are not identical, but their general import is the same: she allegedly brought about the downfall of her ex-husband as a Christian martyr, partly by inflaming the passions of her own brother and partly by encouraging her son to conspire with pagans from the Viking outback in the Isle of Man and the Scottish isles.[24]

Can we believe any of this? I think not. The literary characterization looks very like Shakespeare's treatment of English history. Gormlaith was known to have existed, as a daughter, as a wife and as a mother; authors felt free to do what they liked with her character. A strong-willed woman as an inciter of violence is a recognized literary topos.[25] Donnchadh Ó Corráin has suggested, tentatively, that the lost *Brjáns saga* was composed, in Old Norse, in Dublin *c.*1100, at a time when an Ua Briain was the town's and the kingdom's effective overlord.[26] Would it have been acceptable, supposing this to be true, to blacken the name of a wife of Muirchertach's famous great-grandfather? The answer is that it probably was, because Muirchertach was descended not from Gormlaith's son Donnchad, but from his older half-brother Tadc.[27] Nevertheless the real Gormlaith was presumably living in Dublin in 1014 and may well have witnessed from a distance the progress of the great battle, in company with her son Sigtryggr and her daughter-in-law Sláine.[28] Her brother and her ex-husband were both killed that day, whereas Gormlaith lived on for another sixteen years.

Does she bear comparison with the biblical Jezebel?[29] No one said so at the time or even later, though there were some parallels. Gormlaith was a queen; one of her husbands was killed in a great battle; she accommodated herself, from time to time, to an alternative religion; and she was no doubt in the thick of things for many years. On the other hand, she did not occasion the stoning to death of an innocent man and she herself did not come to a sticky end. Unlike in the case of a small number of Anglo-Saxon and Frankish royal consorts, Gormlaith escaped from, or did not deserve, biblically inspired censure.[30] Instead she became, in the Irish manner, 'a distinct literary entity in her own right'.[31]

Instead we can only assume that she continued to live on in Sigtryggr's household, occupying an honourable social position. Nothing is known for certain of her physical appearance, though the Dublin excavations have yielded an impressive collection of female headcoverings in the form of caps and scarves made of silk or wool.[32] We know, too, that brehon law placed a higher value on the veil worn on the head of a queen.[33] In conventional saga style, 'she was endowed with great beauty and all those attributes which were outside her own control'.[34] On her death in 1030, three contemporary annalists recorded that event, mainly in terms of her motherhood of two kings and without any element of judgment.[35] Finally, where was she buried? Round about then, to the best of our knowledge, another signal event occurred in Dublin: Sigtryggr and a young Irish priest called Dúnán established the Hiberno-Norse diocese of Dublin and founded a cathedral dedicated to the Holy Trinity, known familiarly to us as Christ Church.[36] It is conceivable that this church was founded by Sigtryggr, at least in part, as a royal mausoleum for his mother, who had worked so hard and for so long to promote the interests of this son by her first marriage. At any rate, the probability is that Gormlaith was laid to rest in or near the new cathedral church, whose successor still stands beyond the medieval city wall preserved so impressively in the Wood Quay Venue.

The Farmer's Tale

CHERIE N. PETERS

This tale tells the story of an element of society that is often overlooked. The majority of surviving legal, ecclesiastical and literary sources for Ireland in the eleventh century focus on the people who wrote the texts and the people for whom they were written: the elite of society, the priests and clerics, the warriors and kings. The lower classes entered into the story only as background individuals or flat characters used to move a story along. It is my intention to breathe some life back into these characters – the common farmers who comprised the majority of the population of eleventh-century Ireland.

Farmers in Co. Dublin were low-status members of a hierarchical, kinship-based community who worked exceedingly hard for the survival of their families. These men would have been both arable farmers and animal husbandmen. Their wives would have played the role of small animal herder, child minder, cloth maker and food producer. Their lives would have been anything but easy. In addition to working for their own survival, these farmers would have owed food renders and limited services to their lords (*flathi*), which would have depleted the family stock on a biannual basis. In the early Middle Ages, common farmers could voluntarily become clients (*céle*) to noblemen (who then became their lords) when they inherited land, but not enough livestock or tools to make their farm viable. A noble Irishman's legal status was partially based on how many clients he accrued in this manner. The grant of stock from lords to their clients was repaid twice a year, by way of a hosting once in the summer and once in the winter. The lord was entitled to bring a retinue to feast at each of his client's homes, particularly during the so-called coshering season between

New Year's Day and Shrovetide. These visits were timed specifically when food stocks among poorer farmers were at their lowest: it was after sowing, but before both harvesting and the production of dairy goods.

Most of the life of a commoner would have revolved around his or her farm. The yearly cycle of seeding, planting and harvesting required constant attention, while livestock also had to be cared for and maintained. Cows, pigs, sheep, goats, chickens, dogs and cats had to be fed, corralled and protected from predators, both animal and human. The higher up a farmer was on the social hierarchy the more animals he generally owned. The rhythm of the farming year dominated the lives of these individuals. In February the festival of *Imbolc* was celebrated. One tenth-century scholar called this the 'time that sheep's milk comes', a fanciful explanation for the birth of new animals and the beginning of spring. Originally dedicated to *Brig*, the pagan goddess, it was, by the eleventh century, a celebration of both St Brigid and spring that eventually turned into the Christian celebration of Candlemas. In April farmers began to plant their crops. In May there was the celebration of *Beltaine*, when most farmers drove their cattle up into the hills for summer grazing and it was the main season of dairy production. June was the time when the crops had reached full growth and one ninth-century monastic rule mentioned the celebration of a festival entitled *Féil na n-aireman* ('festival of the ploughmen'). Early August was the start of the harvest. This was celebrated by the festival of *Lugnasad* (pls 3, 4). November was marked by *Samhain*, which signalled the start of winter. All of these various festivals, most of which originated in the pagan world, continued in a Christian one as celebrations of the farming season and allowed farmers to relax from the normal day-to-day drudgery of farm life. At festivals such as these and the yearly assembly (*óenach*) held by kings, various levels of society would have been able to enjoy watching events such as horse-racing and buying and selling at markets that may have included overseas traders and general feasting. Living in a Christian society, work was also suspended on Sundays and saints' days, many of which were also associated with either feasting or fasting.[1]

This routine was the basic template of a farmer's life, but it was not, of course, fixed. The lives of farmers would have been constantly interrupted, and in some cases destroyed, by warring noble factions and increased raiding in the eleventh century. Politics were especially complicated after the death of the high-king Brian Bóruma at the Battle of Clontarf in 1014 and the annalistic records show an increase in raids carried out at this time by the nobility of Ireland on neighbouring and rival territories. Once Brian's triumphs had made it clear to other provincial kings that any man with enough power and supporters could become high-king – a position that before Brian had been held solely by members of the Uí Néill dynasty – every petty king began to fight for his chance at the ultimate seat of power in Ireland. The Hiberno-Norse town of Dublin was a particularly prized possession and, as a result, many political raids and battles were fought in the hinterland. As Poul Holm has discussed above in the Slave's Tale, the spoils of many of these raids included all sorts of moveable goods, but the most common items taken were cattle and people. The annals recorded that in the year 1031 Aedh Ua Néill took 3,000 cows and 1,200 captives from Telach Ócc or modern-day Tullaghoge in Co. Tyrone. (This is probably an exaggerated number designed to flatter Ua Néill, but it nevertheless shows that common farmers were in danger of having their stock and possibly even themselves carried off in a raid.) In that same year the men of Dublin raided Ardbrecáin and took 200 people into captivity. The raiding and destruction of religious settlements, such as Glendalough and Clonmacnoise in 1020, disrupted not only the lives of the religious brethren living there, but also the poor farmers who worked the surrounding settlements and lost not only their crops, but also, in many instances, their lives.

In addition to the chaotic political situation, farmers also had to contend with dangerous natural disasters of the eleventh century. The annals inform us about periodic bouts of snow, hail, rain, wind and disease that beset some of these farmers and made their daily lives that much more perilous. The Annals of the Four Masters note that in the summer of 1022, hail, thunder and lightning played havoc with the country and many men and cattle were destroyed as a result. Although crops were not specifically mentioned in this record, summer was the growing season for the crops and any damage done then would have affected the quality and quantity of the later harvest. Similarly, a 'violent wind' in the autumn of 1077 was noted for causing great damage to the corn crop. The harsh winter of 1047 was catastrophic to both animals and people:

> A great famine came upon the Ulidians, so that they left their territory, and proceeded into Leinster … great snow in this year (the like of which was never seen) … so that it caused the destruction of cattle and wild animals, and the birds of the air and the animals of the sea in general.[2]

Some years there was too much rain and sometimes there were droughts. (The idea that Ireland could at some point have been in drought conditions may seem unlikely to us now, but in the eighth century alone four different periods of drought are mentioned in the annals.) Inclement weather played havoc with the growth and production of crops as well as the maintenance of livestock and it is clear, therefore, that the eleventh century was a very difficult time for anyone to survive, noble and farmer alike. Yet many farmers did manage to survive, despite the onslaught of adverse weather, pestilences, and raiding parties.

I am going to look at three important aspects of a farmer's daily life in this tale – where they lived and the types of house they lived in, the types of clothes they wore and finally the foods they are likely to have eaten – in order to gain a better understanding of what their lives were like. The Old Irish law tracts present a stratified vision of housing, whereby different-sized circular houses were considered appropriate for different ranks in society. The circumferences of these houses ranged from sixteen to twenty-seven feet for common farmers and were most likely surrounded by a circular earthen mound barrier, hence the terms ringfort or *ráth* that have often been applied to these structures. By the eleventh century, some houses were also constructed in the shape of a rectangle, but the reason for this shift, whether due in part to ecclesiastical or Viking influence, remains unclear. The domestic structure and any outhouses or small animal pens were situated within the interior of the settlement. Gardens were most likely not cultivated inside since they could easily have been trampled by the animals kept there. Stock animals were sometimes penned in by post-and-wattle fences. Other animals such as dogs, cats and chickens, however, had freer range within the enclosure.

The house itself would have been constructed with post-and-wattle walls. To make these walls, wooden stakes were placed in the ground with the wattle wrapped around them. If the wall was constructed with two layers, a space was most likely left between them and filled in with straw, moss, grass or heather as an early form of insulation. A hearth was generally located at the centre of the house in order to provide maximum heating for the inhabitants. The law tracts discuss two openings that would have been built into the structure. It is possible that, if the house did not have an opening in the roof to remove it from the hearth, smoke would have escaped from one of these openings so as not to injure the inhabitants. One of these openings most likely had a door attached to it while the other remained open with a lintel above. It has been suggested by some archaeologists and historians that the difference in the two openings could have been due either to wind direction (the door faced the windward side and the lintel faced the leeward side) or to the placement of outbuildings in the yard (the lintel could have allowed convenient access to an outbuilding).[3] A number of beds or couch structures were also generally found in early medieval farming households. These were most likely attached to the wall in some way and supported by two wooden legs. Organic material was used to cushion the beds, and we know that brushwood and meadow grass in particular were used for this. This material would have brought additional unwanted residents to the house, such as lice and fleas.[4] The floors were also strewn with organic material including heather, brushwood, leaves, peat, ash, clay and charcoal. Other organic material found its way to the floors as a by-product of food production: many domestic floors from this period were covered in a variety of refuse including shells, animal bones or burnt grains. All of this, combined with dogs and cats running around inside the house, would probably have led to sanitary conditions that we would now consider intolerable but back then would have been par for the course.

Thus we can picture, perhaps, where farmers lived – now what about what they wore? According to one law tract, most common farmers owned only two garments each, one worn and one new. Although the types of garment considered appropriate for the lower classes were not outlined in the law tracts, most scholars assume they were either the common *brat* ('cloak') and long *léine* ('tunic') that are described so often in historical tales or the shorter *léine* and trousers often displayed on high crosses and in manuscript illuminations as being worn by warriors. Most historians and art historians argue that it is more likely that farmers wore a combination of a shorter *léine* and trousers, since these garments were more comfortable and manoeuvrable. This ease of movement suited people who had an active lifestyle, like warriors or farmers. *Aislinge Meic Conglinne,* a Middle-Irish wonder tale, describes the attire of a lower-class juggler as 'short garments', referring to a short *léine*. It is possible that this short *léine* would have often been accompanied by trousers. They are not mentioned in this tale, however, most likely owing to the fact that the tale mocks the juggler, who is left bare-bottomed. Different types of cloth would have been available in this period, but the two main textiles readily available to individuals of lower status were linen and wool. Even though references to silk threads can be found in the historical records and silken headgear has been found in archaeological excavations of Viking Age Dublin, it is probable that most small farmers would have seen silk only from a distance on the garments of much wealthier nobles.

The colours of these garments could visually signify a person's status in eleventh-century Ireland. The law tracts, for instance, describe the types of clothes children were supposed to wear and different coloured garments distinguished the child of a farmer from that of a king. It was considered acceptable by the jurists for the children of kings and warriors to wear clothes dyed in strong colours such as purple, red, green or blue. The children of farmers, however, had to make do with a more muted palate of black, yellow, brown or dun-coloured. Some early medieval satirists used this association between muted colours and the lower classes to disparage the status of their target:

> You bit of a man, you form of the Devil,
>
> you comb in a larder, you flea-ridden woodcock,
>
> you worn-out lower quern, you fence of yew,
>
> you drink after thirst, you dun-coloured tunic.[5]

These colours could have been achieved through a number of processes. The twelfth-century historian Gerald of Wales noted that the black garments appropriate to people of lower status were the product of black sheep, but since most sheep in Ireland were not black at this time Gerald was probably mistaken, misinformed or possibly intentionally drawing a disparaging connection between black sheep and the 'barbaric' Irish. A nineteenth-century scholar, Joseph C. Walker, argued that the black colour was obtained instead from bogs. He described a process in which vegetables were set with a common mordant from the Middle Ages – urine. The bark of alder, elder or oak trees was also commonly used and could produce a deep black. The yellow garments most often associated with the Irish of late medieval Ireland were dyed with saffron, but there is no evidence to indicate that saffron was readily available in the eleventh century. Instead, *buí mór* ('weld'), a native Irish plant that also produced a strong yellow colour, is likely to have been the source for cloth-dyeing at this time. Although weld does grow wild in Ireland it was often cultivated on waste land or poor pasture and sometimes it was sown under barley. Thus, not only did the resulting colour indicate a person's status, but also the materials used to produce the colour were not commonly thought of as luxurious.

Whether or not a common farmer would also have had a pair of shoes in his possession is a difficult question to answer. A.T. Lucas' remarkable study on footwear in medieval Ireland distinguished a wide array of shoe types, including a very basic one-piece foot-formed rawhide shoe and more intricate leather varieties.[6] Dáire O'Rourke argued that a wrap-around type of ankle-boot was common among the Hiberno-Norse inhabitants of tenth- and eleventh-century Dublin.[7] Some historical sources associate shoes with harvesting and note that they could have been used as a recompense for damage done to the furniture in a farmer's house, but do not specifically describe any farmers wearing shoes. The vast number of shoes found in the early medieval archaeological record, however, indicates that a variety of shoes were produced, from the very simple to the elaborate, and could have been made or purchased by well-to-do farmers or their family members. Thus, the clothing of Irish farmers in eleventh-century Dublin most likely consisted of either a *brat* and *léine* or a short *léine* and trousers, made out of wool and linen respectively, dyed with muted colours and possibly accompanied by a pair of rawhide shoes.

While both wool and cowhides were important in the clothing of farmers, it is perhaps surprising that the meat of these domestic animals played such a small role in their diet. The law tracts described a meagre diet that consisted mainly of small amounts of bread and dairy products. Two types of loaf were produced in early medieval Ireland: one, a loaf baked for a man, was roughly twice the size of the loaf baked for a woman. These loaves could have been made from a number of grains that were cultivated in early medieval Ireland, including wheat, rye, barley and oats. Barley and oats were by far the most common grains, as is evidenced by the plethora of survivals in the archaeological record, and they were subsequently given the lowest ranking in the historical record. One eighth-century law tract, *Bretha Déin Checht* ('The judgments of Dían Cécht'), details a hierarchy that associated particular grains with different ranks of individual and barley and oats are at the bottom of the list:

> A grain of wheat for a supreme king, a bishop and a master poet. A grain of rye for a superior king, an *ánroth* poet ... and a priest ... A grain of red wheat for an *aire túise* ... and for every person of equal status corresponding to him. A grain of barley for an *aire déso* and every person of equal status corresponding to him. A grain of oats for a *bóaire* and every person of equal status corresponding to him. A pea for an *ócaire* ... a bean for a *fer midboth*.[8]

The grains were most likely ground at a mill that farmers could have owned outright or had a shared interest in. It is also possible that a lot of lower-status households ground their own grain in their homes using querns. This task was generally performed by the women of the household and would have taken a great deal of time and effort. Barley and oats do not contain the necessary gluten levels for leavening and as such the loaves made from these grains would have been both flat and dense, perhaps explaining why wheat was considered luxurious and appropriate for a king.

A high proportion of the diet consisted of dairy products such as milk or curds. Milk was most likely obtained from cows, but other domestic milk-producing animals such as sheep and goats provided an alternative. Although neither of these was held in high esteem by medieval authors, goats' milk was valued more highly than sheep's by a twelfth-century legal commentator. Milking the animals was most likely the job of the farmer's wife and children. Oddly, the consumption of butter was regulated according to the jurists. In early medieval Ireland, hospitality – the entertainment and feeding of guests in one's home – was very important and the law tracts describe the types of food a person was entitled to request during these visits based on his or her rank in society. Only certain individuals were entitled to request butter. The youngest and lowest rank of farmers, the *fer midboth* (literally, 'man between two houses'), was not entitled to butter according to the eighth-century law tract, *Críth Gablach* ('branched purchase'). Nevertheless, the farmer just above him in grade and rank, the *ócaire* ('young farmer') was entitled to request butter, but only while on sick maintenance, an early medical practice that was dying out well before the eleventh century. By the eleventh century, this act of caring was generally replaced by a payment. Typically, however, though not all grades were entitled to request butter when visiting another person's table, a farmer's consumption of butter within his own house was not prescribed.

Although the historical sources indicate that meat was, most likely, not an everyday food for farmers, there were clearly times when it was consumed. Beef is discussed in some of the early literature as a food mainly reserved for the upper echelons of society, since it was included in the feasts that clients had to prepare for the lords. For the farmers of Co. Dublin, some of the meat from their livestock probably also went to feed the inhabitants of the Hiberno-Norse town. Game meats, on the other hand, such as wild boar and venison, probably had a higher consumption rate among the lower classes, depending on their proximity to a wooded area. One example of the prevalence of game meats in the farmer's diet comes from a story in the seventh-century *Life of Columba* by Adomnán. In this story, a desperate layman approached Columba and pleaded with him for help in feeding his hungry family. The saint kindly crafted a stake and then blessed it for the layman. When he handed it over to the destitute man, Columba clearly stated that the weapon would kill neither cows nor men but would instead kill only wild animals for his consumption. Following this sage guidance, the poor layman planted the stake in the ground near a section of wood and for a while he and his family never wanted for food. Indeed, he acquired so much meat that he began to sell his surplus to his neighbours. Unfortunately, his defiant wife did not have faith in the saint's promise that the stake would not harm a person and the layman removed the stake from its place near the wood. He and his family ended up back where they started – hungry.[9] Another common food in early medieval Ireland was fish, with salmon and trout being considered extremely valuable by medieval authors. Shellfish, however, was less prized and was consumed on a more general basis by people who lived near water. Given Dublin's proximity to the sea, it is surprising to find that some recent studies on human bones from the area have indicated low levels of marine life in the diet.[10]

In addition to corn, dairy products, wild game and fish, farmers supplemented their diet with various fruits and vegetables, either wild or cultivated. Native plants grew naturally around many settlements in Ireland. Siobhán Geraghty, in her discussion of the plants in Viking Age Dublin, noted that apples, blackberries and even some strawberries grew wild in the surrounding areas and were probably consumed by the inhabitants.[11] Stories from some Old and Middle Irish hagiographical texts demonstrated a high-status preference for cultivated sweet apples, while the native bitter apples that were generally found on common lands were more often consumed by low-status individuals, including farmers. The law tracts also mention vegetables such as onions, dulse (seaweed), wild garlic and leeks. As a result, the diet of farmers in early medieval Ireland was not quite so bland as one might expect.

Thus, if we imagine a married couple, perhaps named Diarmait and Eithne, we can see what the lives of a typical medieval Irish farming family would have been like: Diarmait was a farmer on family lands and Eithne worked at home, in charge of raising their children and their foster-children, but also responsible for milking their cows, grinding the grain and weaving their clothes. On Eithne's trips to festivals, she was distinguishable from her wealthier neighbours by the dun-coloured coarse wool tunic that she wore and possibly her bare feet. As a family, they did own a pair of shoes, but to make this valuable possession last as long as possible they were usually worn by Diarmait only when he was harvesting, or by Eithne if the road in winter was covered by snow or ice. Their house was what we might call chaotic – the whole family in one room, a room in which they prepared, cooked and ate all their meals, a room in which they all slept and which on a windy day was often filled with smoke from the hearth, beside which the cat often slept. Their chickens ran underfoot, pursued in earnest by the dog.

Life for Diarmait and Eithne was often difficult: in their lifetimes they had both known winters where food was short owing to bad harvests; they had family members and neighbours who had been killed defending their homes and family from attacks, and friends who had simply disappeared, perhaps killed, taken hostage or sold abroad as slaves. But the year was not a relentless struggle for survival – births, marriages, saints' days, a successful harvest – all of these provided Diarmait and Eithne with the opportunity to meet and socialize with their neighbours and to celebrate life's small but significant achievements.

Our two hard-working friends, Diarmait and Eithne, and so many of their kind were never named in any annals and there were no sagas written about them, but they were the people who lived through the raids of Irish provincial kings and Vikings, through droughts and pestilences. Despite all that, they had many of the same concerns that we have today – they went to work, supported their families and on their days off enjoyed feasting with friends and loved ones. Though not often given a voice, the farmer has a tale that can resonate from the eleventh century to the present day.

The Tax Collector's Tale

ÁINE FOLEY

Thomas de Crumlin and his contemporaries in late thirteenth-century Ireland would have been aware of the biblical tale involving the tax collector Zacchaeus, who, because of his occupation, was labelled a sinner by his community. The story of Zacchaeus and other references in the New Testament to tax collectors reveal that they were generally despised, and were even compared to prostitutes.[1] Evidence from such texts as the Robin Hood tales suggests that there was no love lost for tax collectors in the Middle Ages, since the sheriff of Nottingham, collector of taxes, is a reviled character. One literary work that did not vilify tax collectors was *The Canterbury Tales*, but this is hardly surprising considering that Chaucer had worked as a tax collector during his long service to the English crown. Chaucer notwithstanding, the general abhorrence of tax collectors was no doubt borne out of the fact that, unlike today, people knew the men who took their taxes. It is hard to know how Thomas de Crumlin's neighbours felt about him, but there is evidence that this dislike of tax collectors existed not solely in works of fiction. In 1326, a London mob murdered Walter de Stapledon, the treasurer of England, and his downfall was undoubtedly a consequence of the burdensome taxes he had inflicted on London's citizens.

Tax collectors may have been perceived as an evil, but they were a necessary evil (pl. 7). For example, it would have been impossible for King Edward I to conduct his wars in Scotland and Wales without collecting taxes, and men like Thomas de Crumlin were required to help collect these duties. The inhabitants of south Co. Dublin would have been very familiar with their local tax collector, since Thomas' family had been in Dublin for at least a century by the time he was appointed. They took their name from the royal manor of Crumlin, just a short walk south of the walls of the medieval city (pls 5, 6). Their 'proper' surname was Russell and contemporary records reveal that they used Russell and de Crumlin interchangeably throughout the thirteenth and fourteenth centuries. This variability in surnames can make members of the family difficult to distinguish in the historical record. They appear prominently in sources from medieval Dublin and, like many of their fellow Dubliners, they may have had familial ties to the canons of the cathedral church of St Patrick. Many clerics came to Dublin in the aftermath of the invasion in 1169 and brought relatives and other followers with them. It was through these clerical connections that many of these newcomers acquired land and settled in Dublin. It is possible that Patrick Russell, parson of the church of Balrothery in north Co. Dublin, was a member of this family, and his association with the cathedral could have been the impetus for their move to Ireland.[2]

Although Thomas' family is associated with the manor of Crumlin, they also held lands elsewhere in Dublin. Osbert Trussell (a possible variation of Russell), who held lands in Wimbletown in Lusk at the end of the twelfth century, may have been one of the first members of the Russell family in Ireland.[3] Osbert is a relatively unusual first name in Ireland, so it is likely that it was a family name and that Osbert de Crumlin, who held lands on this manor a century later, was related to this Osbert Trussell of Wimbletown.[4] Around the same time as Osbert Trussell held lands in north Dublin, William de Crumlin, a relative, was paying the yearly rent of a pound of pepper for land in Crumlin.[5] He paid sixteen pounds in pepper for this property in 1212, which suggests that he was sixteen years in arrears. This indicates that the de Crumlin family had settled in this area by the end of the twelfth century and may even have been there since shortly after the invasion. Though their main interests were now in south Dublin, and subsequent generations continued to pay their annual rent of a pound of pepper for lands in Crumlin, some members of the de Crumlin family continued to hold lands in the northern part of the county. During the middle of the thirteenth century, John de Crumlin granted thirty-seven acres there to Margery de Crumlin – who was most likely his daughter – and her new husband, Richard de Killeich.[6]

The sources indicate that William's lands in Crumlin became the property of one Osbert de Crumlin after William's death. Osbert, probably William's son, appears to have maintained close links with England: a patent letter from 1257 reveals that Osbert Cromelyn of Worcestershire was a knight, since he was granted a 'respite from knighthood' because of his advanced age.[7] This Osbert Cromelyn was possibly the same individual as Osbert de Crumlin of Dublin, because Crumlin is often spelled Cromelyn in medieval records and Osbert de Crumlin would indeed have been an old man by 1257. The argument that these Osberts were one and the same is supported by the fact that the Cromelyns of Worcester appear to have had kinship ties with the Russells of that same county. Russell, as previously mentioned, was an alternative surname for the de Crumlins of Dublin. The connection between these families in England is apparent from the marital ties and the land holdings that we can trace for the Crumlin, Russell and also Hodington families in Worcestershire, all of whom seem to have been related individuals using different surnames. Moreover, a church in the manor of Strensham in the county contains a panelled altar tomb for Sir John Russell, who died in 1556, and it bears the arms not only of the Russell family, but also those of the Hodington and Crumlin families.[8] If Osbert de Crumlin and his namesake in Worcestershire were, in fact, the same individual, the 1257 patent letter reveals a great deal about the social status of the de Crumlin family. As mentioned above, Osbert de Cromelyn of Worcestershire was of knightly status and thus his family could claim to be among the ranks of the lesser nobility, a class that was becoming increasingly more exclusive from the thirteenth century onwards. Osbert's knightly status and his ability to support that status financially was confirmation that the de Crumlin family were people of consequence on both sides of the Irish Sea.

References to the family are sparse for the later thirteenth century and only two de Crumlins appear in the sources. One, Roger de Crumlin, appears in a legal case in 1277 when he was accused of raping a woman named Sara Norreys.[9] It is likely that he was the same person known as

Roger Russell, who appears sporadically in the witness lists of charters dealing with lands in south Dublin from the third quarter of the thirteenth century. Since witnesses for charters were usually drawn from the immediate locality, it is entirely plausible that he was Osbert de Crumlin's son.

The second de Crumlin from this period was Thomas, who first appears in contemporary records in 1276. At this time, Ralph le Sauser accused him of 'violently' depriving him of the custody of his ward (and her inheritance), the unnamed – and underage – daughter and heir of Adam Latimer. Thomas subsequently married her.[10] In order to recoup his losses, Ralph took Thomas to court. He sought the £35 owed to him by the king for the custody of Adam Latimer's lands.[11] This implies that Latimer's daughter was quite a substantial heiress. Undoubtedly, this marriage had the potential to greatly enhance Thomas' position in his locality. The lands and chattels of the newlyweds were confiscated until Thomas agreed to appear in court. The outcome of the case is unknown, but ultimately it was not too detrimental to Thomas. He was included on a jury of the leading knights and free tenants of Dublin in 1284, which suggests that his lands were back in his possession by this date.[12] Thomas de Crumlin found himself in trouble on more than one occasion. In 1286 during Easter term, he was fined ten marks for trespass but, unfortunately, the source does not specify the nature of the misdemeanour. Ten marks was an extremely large amount of money at the time and therefore the offence must have been a relatively serious transgression. It was possibly related to his abduction of Adam Latimer's daughter. In the same year, he was fined one mark for contempt. Again the reference is vague, but it may have been an attempt by Thomas to avoid public office or jury service, since this was a common reason that people received fines at this time.[13] Though Thomas was fined on several occasions, we never discover the exact nature of these crimes or misdemeanours. Nevertheless, if he had the means to pay his fines, it suggests that he was reasonably prosperous.

Thomas' brushes with the law should not be exaggerated; clearly he was also a trusted member of the community. This is borne out by the fact that he served as both a juror and a tax collector.[14] At the end of the thirteenth century, he was responsible for collecting the fifteenth; this was a tax that was assessed on a fraction of the value of an individual's movable goods. In England, this fraction often varied, but after 1334 it became standardized at one-fifteenth of the value of a taxpayer's movable property.[15] The fifteenth appears to have been the norm in Dublin at least half a century before this date. In the 1290s Thomas de Crumlin and Geoffrey Harold collected this tax in the Vale of Dublin on several occasions.[16] The late thirteenth century marked the apex of Ireland as a source of revenue for the English crown. Edward I put extreme financial pressure on the colony as a means to fund his Scottish and Welsh wars, and men like Thomas de Crumlin helped to facilitate these military operations. His value as a royal servant explains why he held the farm of the king's demesne in Crumlin. The pitfalls of public service are revealed by a memoranda roll entry from 1310–11 wherein, two decades after their time as tax collectors, Geoffrey Harold and Thomas – or rather his heir John de Crumlin – still owed the considerable sum of £103 18s. 4d.[17] This debt presumably arose from the failure of Thomas and Geoffrey to collect the amount of tax that the king and his officials in Ireland expected from the county. Thus, they were personally liable for the shortfalls.

Thomas de Crumlin held the farm of the king's demesne in Crumlin up to 1290, when it was granted to an English official called Henry de Compton. Thomas' fellow tenants on the manor of Crumlin, as well as the tenants living on the royal manors of Newcastle Lyons and Saggart, rallied around him and de Compton was met with fierce opposition.[18] How the tenants of these three manors impeded Compton from enjoying the grant of lands and the pleas and perquisites of their courts is not specified, but eventually the crown was forced to grant the demesne lands to the tenants of Crumlin manor. There does seem to have been a subtle power shift within the community. Up to this point, at least throughout the 1280s when the records begin to become relatively abundant, Thomas de Crumlin was almost exclusively paying the rent. After 1292, however, we find several different tenants paying the rent into the exchequer.[19] Perhaps the tenants who had found themselves capable of standing up to Henry de Compton were now also able to stand up to Thomas de Crumlin. Additionally, Thomas had just become the tax collector for the Vale of Dublin and relations with his fellow tenants may have become less friendly because of his associations with this unpopular office. It may simply have been the case that his administrative duties prevented him from giving his full attention to running the royal demesne. Thomas did occasionally pay the rent of the manor during the 1290s, but it was usually in conjunction with his son Adam.

As well as the money rents he paid for the manor of Crumlin, Thomas paid one pound of pepper a year for the plot of land that had once belonged to Osbert and William de Crumlin.[20] His parcel of land was separate and distinct from the much larger one carucate and eight acres that Thomas was granted on the king's royal demesne.[21] According to a memoranda roll entry for 1309–10, this plot consisted of two messuages and twenty-nine acres.[22] A messuage was a dwelling house and outbuildings, with a small parcel of land assigned for its use.[23] As well as the lands already mentioned, Thomas de Crumlin paid rents for other holdings in Crumlin.[24] Though the carucate and eight acres of the royal demesne were in Thomas' hands only temporarily, the fact that both of his sons held property on the manor suggests that they had other substantial landholdings there. While Thomas' son John inherited Osbert's plot, his other son Adam held almost seventy acres sown with wheat and oats in Crumlin in 1304.[25] Various members of the family owned lands in Coolock, Artane and Stratbaly, in north Co. Dublin, as well as Ballymakelly near Newcastle Lyons and Donore, near modern-day Cork Street in the liberties.

John de Crumlin was probably Thomas' older son, who could expect to inherit the bulk of his father's property. His younger son Adam went into royal service, possibly since he did not expect to inherit much land from his father. Even if Thomas' property was to be divided between his sons, as sometimes was the practice in Ireland, Adam may still have had to seek an income and ways to acquire more land so that he could hold as much as his father did and maintain his status.

Adam became sheriff of Dublin in 1299.[26] The sheriff was the most important royal official in the county and he served as a conduit between the English crown and the local community. Increasingly, this office was the reserve of members of the local elite and its holders came from the most politically prominent families. While Adam de Crumlin did not come from the highest echelons of this society, his qualifications for this office are clear. His family had established themselves in the locality over a century earlier and their parcels of lands scattered across the county added up to a substantial landholding. Moreover, they already had a history of being involved in royal service. Thomas' stint as tax collector for the Vale of Dublin meant that Adam already had some familiarity with the exchequer. In fact, his involvement with the office of sheriff of Dublin dated back to at least 1290 when he served as sheriff's clerk.[27]

Adam's term as sheriff of Dublin marked the family's apex within the county. Future generations did not appear so prominently in contemporary records. He appears to have been the last person in his family to serve as an administrator at the county level, though his brother John did serve as provost of Crumlin, just as his father had before him.[28] John, who is usually referred to as John Russell, though he is occasionally called de Crumlin, first appears in the records in 1301 and he frequently paid the rent of Crumlin manor in the early years of the fourteenth century.[29] He was dead by 1317 when his lands in Crumlin passed into the hands of his son Ralph.[30] A memoranda roll entry from 1309 mentions that Adam's heir was Richard de Crumlin and he was probably deceased by this time.[31] Neither Ralph nor Richard features so prominently in the sources as their forebears.

The de Crumlin family played a vital part in the colonization and administration of Co. Dublin. They held lands in Dublin from the twelfth century. They even had claims to knighthood. While most members of the family were content to build up their landholdings during the thirteenth century, Thomas was the first to pursue administrative office and his son Adam followed in his footsteps. Thomas was an important man in his community, responsible for collecting the king's revenue. Adam built on his father's successes and as sheriff was responsible for overseeing the judicial and military activities of the county. During his term of office, he was substantially responsible for the financial wellbeing of the crown, as well as upholding local law and order. He probably also used the office for personal gain. He certainly acquired several parcels of land at around the same time that he served as sheriff. Although Thomas' sons Adam and John feature prominently in contemporary sources, his grandchildren Ralph and Richard are barely afforded a mention at all. Though it is possible that the Russells of Newcastle Lyons are a branch of this family that survived, at least down to the sixteenth century, they are no longer to be found in the manor of Crumlin. It is possible that the family survived through the female line and married into other local families, but the evidence suggests that the de Crumlin family had reached its zenith in the thirteenth century.

The Archdeacon's Tale

MARGARET MURPHY

My tale concerns a man called Nicholas de Clere, who held the position of archdeacon of Dublin from 1287 to 1303 and who was also treasurer of Ireland from 1285 to 1291. It is a cautionary tale, in many ways, of a man who achieved much in his career but ended his life in disgrace. The tale also allows us to examine an ecclesiastical office that, although obscure to many of us now, was very real and familiar to medieval people.

The archdeacon was a diocesan official – each diocese had an archdeacon and many had more than one. He was often called *oculus episcopi* ('the bishop's eye') because in many ways he functioned as the deputy or the substitute for the bishop, carrying out a range of administrative and financial duties. The archdeacon also had a special duty to oversee the moral behaviour and manners of both the lesser clergy and the laity, which meant that he kept a close eye on what was going on in his diocese. The archdeacon was supposed to refer the most serious infractions of canon law to the bishop's court for judgment but he also had the right to prosecute lesser offences in his own court. Therefore, the archdeacon's eyes were on the diocese, seeking out bad behaviour and bringing those accused to justice. Geoffrey Chaucer provides a striking and humorous vignette of an archdeacon in the tale told by the friar in *The Canterbury Tales*:

> In my own district once there used to be
> A fine archdeacon, one of high degree,
> Who boldly did the execution due
> On fornication and on witchcraft too.

He goes on to detail all the other offences that the archdeacon sought out – defamation, non-payment of tithes, breaches of contract – before concluding:

> But he could boast
> That lechery was what he punished most.[1]

The archdeacon's punishments were invariably of a financial nature. Chaucer's friar tells us that, before the bishop caught offenders with his crook, their names had all been written down in the archdeacon's book. Mention of the archdeacon's book makes one long for the survival of such a manuscript from the medieval Dublin archdeaconry! Another famous literary archdeacon is Theophilus Grantly in Anthony Trollope's *The Warden*. Archdeacon Grantly was a pompous individual, ever conscious of the rights and privileges of the church. He was not a popular man, particularly with the ordinary working folk of his diocese. He got angry if he felt that his dignity was not recognized and even his wife addressed him as 'archdeacon'.

Archdeacons have been part of the structure of the Christian church since at least the fourth century, initially attached to monasteries and subsequently to cathedrals. It was, however, not until the late eleventh and twelfth centuries that they took on their important and distinctive roles in diocesan organization. The introduction of the office of archdeacon to the dioceses of Ireland has been attributed to the Anglo-Normans and is generally seen as one of their innovations in the sphere of ecclesiastical administration. It is possible, however, that the office was introduced before the Anglo-Normans arrived as part of the twelfth-century reform of the Irish church that saw the establishment of the territorial dioceses. The earliest specific mention of an archdeacon of Dublin appears in 1185. Thereafter, archdeacons are mentioned in diocesan and provincial legislation and their role in the diocese developed. The legislation of a mid-thirteenth-century diocesan synod urged rectors of churches to be vigilant concerning public conduct and to bring any aberration or excess to the attention of the archdeacon. The legislation further stated that the archdeacon was to ensure that the parochial clergy were in the correct orders and of approved life and education. The archdeacon had several mechanisms to assist him in the carrying out of these duties.

We know that the archdeacon held a number of chapters or gatherings each year, which the lower clergy were obliged to attend and at which he carried out his activities in the sphere of correction of the clergy. The canons of St Patrick's were granted the privilege that the priests in their prebendal churches were obliged to attend only two archidiaconal chapters each year, suggesting that there were more than this. The archdeacon also performed an annual visitation of the parish churches in his diocese. His arrival was much dreaded because it was during these visits that he collected his procurations or payments from the parochial clergy.

The archdeacon had his own court that heard cases concerning the moral conduct of laity and clergy. A controversial aspect of his jurisdiction was that the archdeacon was entitled to keep the revenue from the fines he imposed in his court. Many people thought that it was this benefit that accounted for the ruthless zeal that many archdeacons displayed in hunting down even minor infractions of canon law. Giraldus Cambrensis, well known for his descriptions of Ireland and the Irish, had some harsh things to say about archdeacons – even though he was one himself. He claimed that the office was wholly given over to rapacity and that the name archdeacon 'rings in some men's ears with a sound as horrible as that of arch-devil; for the devil steals men's souls but the archdeacon steals their money'.[2]

The role of the archdeacon in the diocese put him in a special position in relation to the cathedral church, or in the case of Dublin, the cathedral churches. From the early thirteenth century, the archdeacon of Dublin held a prebend in St Patrick's Cathedral. This gave him a source of income distinct from the payments due from his archidiaconal duties. By the 1270s the archdeacon of Dublin held the valuable prebend of Taney along with its dependent churches of Donnybrook, Kilgobbin and Rathfarnham. The archdeacon enjoyed a good relationship with St Patrick's, probably helped by the fact that one of the privileges enjoyed by the canons in their prebends was that these churches would be free from the archdeacon's visitation and most importantly the procurations he levied at these times. The other cathedral, Christ Church, did not have this privilege and this caused bad feelings and aggravation between Christ Church and the archdeacon of Dublin. This was compounded by the fact that Christ Church claimed the tithes of the church of Rathfarnham, part of the archdeacon's prebend. The relationship between the two parties reached an all-time low in the 1320s when the archdeacon excommunicated the prior and the entire convent for refusing to pay his procurations during visitation of their dependent churches. Some of the archdeacon's other functions could involve him in disputes with religious houses. He had the right to preside over the ceremonies installing heads of religious houses and, as the archbishop's deputy, he claimed the right to administer the spiritualities or ecclesiastical possessions of a diocese during a vacancy.

What sort of man became an archdeacon, in particular an archdeacon of Dublin, in the thirteenth century? The renowned ecclesiastical historian A. Hamilton Thompson, author of a work on diocesan administration, wrote in 1943 that there was no ecclesiastical office in which a man was more able to make money and less hampered by purely spiritual concerns than an archdeaconry. This is reflected in the type of men who held the office. Most were practical men of affairs, involved in legal and financial matters, royal chaplains or members of the household clergy of bishops who were themselves royal agents. To be granted an archdeaconry was a sign that one was progressing up the ladder of ecclesiastical promotion and possibly heading for episcopal office. Several of the men who held the archdeaconry of Dublin in the medieval period went on to become bishops in Ireland. Archdeacons needed a legal education in order to be able to deal with the intricacies of matrimonial and testamentary law and most would have had a university education. Such an education was expensive and many archdeacons would have started their careers in debt, particularly as there was no university in Ireland at this time and many clerics would have had to live abroad during the course of their studies. It is not surprising then that they exploited any opportunities for profit.

This brings us to Nicholas de Clere. We do not know much about Nicholas' early career. His name suggests a link with Hampshire in England and the medieval settlements of High Clere or King's Clere. He starts to appear in the records in the 1270s when he was a royal clerk and was beginning to accumulate ecclesiastical benefices. This was a typical start to an archdeacon's career. He held a prebend in the king's chapel within the castle of Nottingham and was appointed custodian of the manor and castle of Taunton in Somerset as well as having interests in Devon and Southampton. He had a connection with the diocese of Exeter where he held two prebends and was custodian of the temporalities of that diocese in 1280. That means he was in charge of the temporal possessions of the diocese following the death of a bishop and before the appointment of a new bishop. In this period, the king took those possessions – property, manors and the like – into his own hands and enjoyed the profits while appointing an official, in this case Nicholas, to act as custodian. In May 1282 Nicholas was appointed as collector of the tax or subsidy granted by the clergy to the king in the archdiocese of Canterbury and the dioceses of Rochester, Chichester and London.

A pattern is emerging of a royal clerk, particularly skilled and experienced in the financial side of ecclesiastical administration. In September 1284 Nicholas was sent to examine customs accounts in Ireland and also to take custody of the temporalities of the archbishopric of Dublin, which was vacant following the death of Archbishop John de Derlington. De Derlington, a prominent Dominican, had been appointed archbishop of Dublin five years previously but had never set foot in his diocese. He was on his way to visit Dublin for the first time when he fell ill and died in the summer of 1284. Nicholas administered the temporalities for a year until they were handed over to John de Sandford, the archbishop-elect. De Clere was instructed to pay over the issues of the diocese to the king's clerks so that they could be used for the walling of certain towns and castles in Wales. This was during the time when King Edward I was engaged in his war against the Welsh princes and was building several castles in Wales. Nicholas performed this task to the king's satisfaction, sending large sums of money (1,600 marks) as well as victuals worth over £150 to Wales from the issues of the vacant archbishopric.

Nicholas was busy in other ways also. He was heading a major enquiry into the state of the Irish exchequer. This enquiry was extended, apparently at his request, into an examination of the entire administration and the conduct of the king's ministers in Ireland. As a result of this, a damning report of the exchequer was published and charges of misconduct were laid against the treasurer and justiciar. At the time these two positions were held by a single individual, Stephen de Fulbourn (bishop of Waterford and later archbishop of Tuam). De Fulbourn was dismissed and in August 1285 Nicholas was appointed treasurer in his place. Less than a year after he arrived in Ireland, de Clere was holding one of the most important positions in the administration of the lordship and commanding an annual salary of £40 (pl. 9).

His ecclesiastical career was also progressing and he started to accumulate benefices in Ireland such as the churches of Lochsewdy in Co. Westmeath and Rathmegan in Co. Kildare. In 1286 or 1287 he was appointed to the archdeaconry of Dublin by Archbishop John de Sandford. De Sandford himself was very involved in the Irish administration. He had held the important position of escheator, the official in charge of accounting to the exchequer for lands and possessions taken into the king's hands for various reasons. These reasons included the death of a landowner leaving an heir who was a minor, the deaths of bishops leaving vacancies and the confiscation of lands of those accused of treachery towards the king. De Sandford would have worked closely with Nicholas during the latter's time as custodian of the archbishopric of Dublin. It is worth noting that de Sandford's department was the only part of the administration to escape unscathed from the enquiry set in train by de Clere. Was the gift of the archdeaconry perhaps an acknowledgment on the part of the new archbishop that de Clere had done him a service?

From a papal letter of 1289 we learn that before he was promoted to the archdeaconry, de Clere was not in holy orders and he had not received a papal dispensation to allow him to hold the churches of Lochsewdy and

Rathmegan. This again is typical of the times, as royal clerks frequently held ecclesiastical benefices without being ordained. A payment to the papal curia ensured a dispensation and a priest was appointed for a small sum to look after the church in question while the clerk pocketed most of the issues. Nicholas was reprimanded for failing to get the dispensation rather than for failing to be in holy orders. He was subsequently ordained, probably at the time he was appointed archdeacon. Since part of the archdeacon's job was to ensure that parochial clergy were ordained, Nicholas could hardly have remained out of orders himself. The papal indulgence he received at this time allowed him to hold on to his other benefices and did not require him to return the moneys he had received from them, but he was instructed to spend £68 on the upkeep of the churches in his benefices.

Everything was going well for Nicholas. His brother William, another royal clerk, came over to Ireland and was appointed deputy treasurer in 1289. Nicholas, however, did not enjoy the fruits of his promotions for very long. In 1290 at a parliament in Westminster, a large number of complaints were made against him in his role as Irish treasurer. It is clear that many of these complaints were made by relatives and friends of the previous treasurer Stephen de Fulbourn (who had died in 1288). The charges were sent to the Irish justiciar and council for investigation. The justiciar was John de Sandford, archbishop of Dublin, and Nicholas might have expected a sympathetic hearing. However, de Sandford was replaced as justiciar in September 1290, apparently at his own request. Did he perhaps not have the stomach to preside over an enquiry into the activities of his colleague and archdeacon? Was he afraid of what might emerge about his own conduct? In any case, de Stanford stood down as justiciar and took himself off to England; accordingly he was not present when the charges against Nicholas were heard in Dublin. These charges related to his levying of fines, his accounting procedure and his propensity to have people arrested and their goods confiscated. Nicholas denied everything of course, but the jury worked on the basis that there is no smoke without fire. He was removed from the office of treasurer and a rigorous audit of his accounts was undertaken.

Much detailed evidence relating to this audit survives and it gives a unique insight into the workings of the Irish exchequer and the corruption that undoubtedly did go on. Where Nicholas' answers to the charges are preserved, they reveal him to be an astute and even humorous man and obviously determined to hold onto his position. One man complained that he was unfairly fined by the treasurer and challenged the impartiality of the jury, which found him guilty saying that it was composed of clerks and members of the treasurer's household. Nicholas replied that in that case everyone in Ireland could be challenged as all were subject to the treasurer and the exchequer. His bravado, however, did him no good. The auditors recorded that this was more evidence of 'the low cunning of the man which is like that of a thief'.[3]

Once news got around that the treasurer was under investigation, the floodgates opened and complaints came in thick and fast. For example, the executors of the will of John de Derlington claimed that Nicholas had taken goods to the value of £431 17s. 101/2d. from the former archbishop's personal possessions. Others complained that, while he was sending goods over to Wales to aid the king's war effort, he had been creaming off the profits. Nicholas' brother William also came under the spotlight. He was charged with presumptuously entering into the exchequer and erasing information from the rolls of that department. It appears that he was fiddling the books, whether to help his brother or save his own skin is not clear.

At the end of the audit, Nicholas was accused of grave transgressions against the king and was committed to the Fleet Prison in London in 1292. It was judged that he owed in excess of £700 to the crown. The archbishop of Dublin and the bishops of the many dioceses in which Nicholas held benefices were ordered to put up for sale all his ecclesiastical goods and the fruits of his benefices, while the treasurer and barons of the exchequer in Dublin were commanded to seize all his lay goods and chattels in Ireland and put them up for sale. The proceeds of these sales were to be paid into the exchequer to offset Nicholas' arrears. From 1294 onwards, the issues of Nicholas' ecclesiastical offices, including the archdeaconry of Dublin, were recorded in the rolls of the Irish exchequer. In some years these issues were very considerable, begging the question of why, when he was in receipt of these issues, Nicholas still felt the need to line his pockets illegally. Perhaps he had lived beyond his means, run into debt or greased too many palms in his ascent to power.

In 1297 Nicholas was granted permission to leave the Fleet Prison in London provided that he could find twelve people to stand surety for him and that he pay a fine of 500 marks to the king. Unhappily, Nicholas could not find people prepared to stand for him. He claimed that if he was allowed to travel to Ireland, he could find people to vouch for him and he could also find the means to pay the fine to the king. He was allowed to travel to Ireland and the Irish exchequer was advised that, if Nicholas could not find sureties, he was to be readmitted to prison. In 1299 Nicholas de Clere was in prison in Dublin Castle, which means that, despite his confidence, he could not find a sufficient number of people to vouch for him in Ireland. It seems that Nicholas remained in prison until his death in 1303. He continued to hold the archdeaconry of Dublin, the issues of which were diverted into the Irish exchequer. After Nicholas' death William de Clere managed to clear himself of association with his brother's debts and partially rehabilitated his own career.

Although Nicholas held the office of archdeacon of Dublin for fifteen years, there is scant evidence of his performing the pastoral duties of that office. In this, however, he was no different from countless other archdeacons. The medieval church was characterized by a spirit of delegation. In the thirteenth century the office of the archdeacon's official, or deputy, emerged and it is to this largely anonymous individual that the designation *oculus episcopi* more correctly belongs. During Nicholas' imprisonment and probably before his fall from grace it was his official who carried out the real work of the archdeacon. Nicholas' successor as archdeacon of Dublin was a fifteen-year-old papal appointee, suggesting that the archdeacon's official continued to perform the duties of that office in Dublin.

John of Salisbury, a late twelfth-century author, diplomat and bishop, tells us about a question that was much debated in his time: can an archdeacon get into heaven? He certainly did not think so and perhaps, having heard this tale of an archdeacon of Dublin, the reader may not think so either.

The Crusader's Tale

EDWARD COLEMAN

The crusades drew support and recruits from all over Europe and the armies that marched to the Holy Land in the twelfth and thirteenth centuries were what today would be called 'multi-national forces'. The crusaders often referred to themselves collectively as Franks, no doubt because many of them came from French-speaking lands that included the kingdom of England and the lordship of Ireland. Two kings of England took the cross and fought in the East with many of their nobles: Richard the Lionheart, who was probably the most famous of all medieval crusaders (1190–2), and, a century later, Richard's great-nephew Edward I (1272–4). The impact of the crusades in Ireland appears to have been slight in the twelfth century, but taking the cross was officially preached on the island from the early 1200s. Thereafter, Irish chroniclers recorded crusading campaigns and celebrated successes; substantial funds were raised in Ireland to support the crusades; men from Ireland took the cross, fought in the Holy Land and in some cases died there. In short, Ireland played a full and active part in the wider crusading movement. What follows is the story of just one of these crusaders, William Fitzroger, but his life should be seen against the backdrop of the wider Irish contribution.[1]

William Fitzroger was the prior, which is to say chief official, of the order of the Knights of St John of Jerusalem in Ireland, c.1274–96. He was therefore, in effect, a professional crusader. His order, more commonly known as the Knights Hospitaller, had been created in the early twelfth century in the wake of the First Crusade and the establishment of the Crusader states; it was given papal approval by Pope Paschal II in 1113.[2] Together with the other major crusading order, the Knights Templar, the Hospitallers were tasked with protecting the Christian shrines of the Holy Land and the pilgrims who visited them. Both Templars and Hospitallers developed as hybrid military-monastic organizations, borrowing their constitution, lifestyle and even dress from pre-existing monastic orders. Like monks, they lived a cloistered life and took vows of celibacy and obedience; unlike monks they also engaged in armed combat. They formed the elite troops of the crusader armies in the East and built numerous castles, several of which survive as impressive ruins. Back at home in Europe, they established a network of bases, sometimes called commanderies or preceptories, to facilitate recruitment, provide hospitality and manage the extensive estates that they acquired through pious donations in support of the crusades.

The Knights Hospitaller are first documented in Ireland in the 1170s and it seems certain that they arrived with the first Anglo-Norman settlers.[3] They certainly benefited from the patronage of several figures associated with the invasion and conquest, most notably Richard de Clare, or Strongbow, who donated the land in Kilmainham, west of Dublin, that became the order's headquarters on the island. The original foundation document of Kilmainham is lost, but it is mentioned in a court case held to resolve a dispute between the Hospitallers and the citizens of Dublin in 1261. This text notes that Strongbow's grant was confirmed by King Henry II, whose death in 1189 provides a *terminus ad quem* for its date, though the original grant must have been made before 1176, the year of Strongbow's death. The Hospitallers were therefore in Ireland from the very beginning of the Anglo-Norman conquest and settlement.[4] The knights who came to Ireland may well have had connections to Wales where the de Clare family had patronized the order in the generation before Strongbow.[5] In the later decades of the twelfth century the Hospitallers acquired additional possessions in Cos Carlow, Cork, Limerick and Wexford. Confirmations issued by King John in 1200 and Pope Innocent III in 1212 regularized their position in the lordship.[6] The papal confirmation lists around 140 properties in Ireland, including estates, churches and chapels, although it is not clear how the order came to hold most of these. Subsequently, whenever the knights became embroiled in disputes with individuals or local communities over their lands and rights – which was often – they could usually count on the support of the crown and they received favourable judgments in several court cases. A good example was their long-running and acrimonious dispute with the citizens of Dublin over fishing and milling rights on the River Liffey, which lasted for several decades in the thirteenth century.

The succession of priors of the order of the Hospital in Ireland can be traced with reasonable accuracy from the late twelfth century. William Fitzroger is the tenth known holder of the office. It is important to note that the Hospitaller priory of Ireland was independent of the English priory, which had its headquarters in Clerkenwell, London. This arrangement was different from that of Templars, whose master in Ireland was subject to his English counterpart. It meant that William Fitzroger had a greater level of responsibility and higher status within his order, and also that the English crown had to deal directly with him concerning Ireland. His dual role as member of the order and servant of the crown is a crucial part of his tale, as we shall see. Both of the military orders worked closely with the royal administration in the lordship during the long reign of Henry III (1216–72). On several occasions the Hospitaller prior and Templar master were called upon to audit the royal accounts, a role that was commonly exercised by members of the military orders in England in this period. The knights were held to be well suited to this task, firstly because they were members of an independent body and owed loyalty to the pope rather than the king. Secondly, they had the advantage of extensive experience in handling large amounts of money donated in Europe and then transferred to the East for the crusades. For the same reason, they were often charged with the custodianship of royal taxes collected in Ireland (both for the crusades and for other purposes) and with the delivery of this money to the royal treasury in England.[7] Several members of the military orders also held important royal offices in Ireland during this period – for example, Stephen de Fulbourn, a brother Hospitaller who emerged as a major figure in the administration during the 1270s and 1280s, serving successively as treasurer, deputy justiciar and justiciar. He went on to become the bishop of Waterford and then archbishop of Tuam, but his career was dogged by accusations of corruption and nepotism that ultimately prompted the king to order a judicial enquiry.[8] The Hospitallers were also employed by the crown in military operations against the Gaelic Irish and it is in this capacity that William Fitzroger comes into view.

English control of Ireland had significantly weakened during the thirteenth century. Certain parts of the country were known as particular centres of opposition to the settlers and one of these was the Wicklow Mountains, an area uncomfortably close to the seat of the royal government in Dublin. Consequently, the crown devoted considerable effort and resources towards 'pacifying' Wicklow, to use the language of official royal documents. The O'Toole and O'Byrne families had been identified as particularly troublesome foes and in 1274 a royal expedition was organized with the aim of quelling their uprising and sending out a message to other would-be insurgents. The initiative for this undertaking came from the justiciar; that is, the king's chief representative in Ireland. At the time this post was held by Geoffrey de Geneville, a close companion of King Edward I who had accompanied him on crusade to the East a few years earlier. It may not therefore be a coincidence that this ex-crusader appointed a professional crusader to lead his force – William Fitzroger, prior of the Hospital of St John in Ireland. As it turned out, the expedition in the Wicklow Mountains was something of a debacle. Fitzroger and his men were ambushed in Glenmalure and many were killed (fig. 8.1). He himself was captured but was released shortly afterwards as part of an exchange of prisoners and probably on payment of a ransom.[9]

Fitzroger's role as a leader of this royal expedition in Wicklow in 1274, albeit a rather inglorious one, provides us with a context for a message sent by Edward I to the prior in the following year. This is contained in a letter patent – an order issued in the king's name by his chancery that would have been unsealed but with the king's great wax seal attached as authentication[10] – dated 27 June 1275. The tone of the missive is censorious:

> Although you [William Fitzroger] have been ordered several times by us [Edward I] to return to Ireland without delay (for the good of

8.1 Glenmalure, from W.H. Bartlett, N.P. Willis and J. Stirling Coyne, *The scenery and antiquities of Ireland*, vol. ii (London, 1842), p. 176.

the crown and the entire land of Ireland), you pretended that as you had been summoned by your superior Hugh Revel, master of your order in the Holy Land, to report to him personally, and as you could not disobey this summons or break your oaths and promises of obedience, you have not been able to comply with our above-mentioned order.[11]

It would seem that Fitzroger was not in Ireland at this time since he was ordered to return there. His whereabouts are not exactly clear but it is a reasonable guess, on the basis of the text of the letter, that he was in England preparing to depart for the Holy Land. The prior had evidently ignored the royal command to return to Ireland, which was a serious matter; moreover he had done so 'several times' according to the letter. His justification for his actions was that the king's command conflicted with one from his superior in the order of the Hospital, Master Hugh Revel. Edward I, however, appears to have been unimpressed by this response and threatened that if William did not return immediately to Ireland all the possessions of the Knights Hospitaller in the island would be confiscated by the crown.

That there was a disagreement here – we might even call it a stand-off – between the king and the Hospitaller prior of Ireland can hardly be in doubt. But why had it come about? Was William Fitzroger really 'pretending' that he had been called to the Holy Land or was the summons genuine? If it was genuine, why did the grand master of the order require the presence of the prior of Ireland in the East? And why did King Edward I want William to return to Ireland as soon as possible instead? In attempting to answer such questions we may gain a better understanding not only of the reasons that lay behind the rift between the king and William Fitzroger in 1275, but also of the role played by the Hospitallers in the lordship of Ireland and by the Irish knights in the wider history of the order and the crusades.

The notion that William Fitzroger 'pretended' to have received a summons to crusade in the East in order to avoid returning to Ireland, which was favoured by earlier scholars such as Caesar Litton Falkiner, ultimately derives from the translation of the word *praetendistis* in the text of King Edward's letter contained in H.S. Sweetman's *Calendar of documents relating to Ireland.* However, *praetendistis* can also be translated with the more neutral meaning of 'claimed', and in reality it seems highly unlikely that the Irish prior would have fabricated a communication from the master of his order.[12] Furthermore, Edward promised to excuse Fitzroger to the master, which would be decidedly odd if the king believed that the prior had invented the order from his superior. Thus, on balance, it would seem that the summons to the Holy Land was probably genuine. In any case, it makes little difference whether William 'pretended' or merely 'claimed' that he had been ordered to go to the East; either way he could hardly have done so out of a desire for a quiet life. Although he had recently suffered the trauma and indignity of capture and ransom at the hands of the Gaelic Irish in Glenmalure, the prospects for a sojourn in the East were certainly no better. Indeed, the situation on the crusade frontier was so dire that it would have been a case of out of the frying pan and into the fire.

By 1275 the crusades had been ongoing for the best part of two centuries. The First Crusade (1095–9) achieved the spectacular and unexpected success of capturing the holy city of Jerusalem itself, and in the wake of this victory the so-called Crusader states were established. But this in turn created the problem of defending the territories gained against overwhelming odds; ultimately, there could only be one outcome. Despite the consolidation of the crusader presence through castle building, the efforts of the military orders on the battlefield, and the launching of further crusades from Europe in support of the resident crusaders, the situation had become critical. By the late thirteenth century the crusaders were clinging on to the last-remaining strip of coastline around the strategic port of Acre in addition to a few isolated strongholds.

One by one the last remaining bulwarks of crusader power were captured. In 1271 one of the largest, most strongly defended and impressive of all crusader castles – Krak des Chevaliers in the county of Tripoli – fell to the Mamluk sultan Baybars. Krak des Chevaliers was a Hospitaller castle; indeed, it was probably the most important fortress of the order in Holy Land and had been occupied continually since the 1140s (fig. 8.2). Its loss was therefore a major setback, even though it was not unexpected. The rapidly deteriorating situation there had been outlined in a letter written three years earlier in 1268:

> For the last eight years we have had no supplies at all from the kingdom of Jerusalem … All the Muslims are now turned on our castles of Krak des Chevaliers and Margat and the sultan is threatening them greatly. You can be in no doubt that we are depressed by our sorrows and anxieties.[13]

It is of interest to note that this letter was written by Hugh Revel, that is to say the same master of the Hospitallers from whom William Fitzroger later claimed he had received a summons to the East in 1275. Furthermore, the letter was addressed to King Edward I of England, whose command to return to Ireland Fitzroger disobeyed on account of his crusading obliga-

8.2 Krak des Chevaliers, Syria (© Abdulhadi Najjar).

tions. Edward himself was far from being indifferent to the crusades despite the clash between the king and the Hospitaller prior of Ireland over this issue. In 1270, two years after receiving Hugh Revel's letter, the king took the cross and set out for the Holy Land with his brother Edmund to bring relief to the beleaguered forces. He remained there for a further two years (1270–2) conducting small-scale operations, strengthening fortifications and engaging in diplomacy.[14] On his return to England he continued to follow events in the East closely and to lend his support. A new crusade was announced at the Second Council of Lyon in July 1274 and preached in England; Edward received another letter from Hugh Revel updating him on the situation in 1275, the very year that he refused Fitzroger permission to travel to the East. Edward therefore had a keen personal interest in crusading and experience of conditions in the Holy Land. He must have been fully aware of the difficulties facing the resident crusaders and in particular the military orders who were on the front line. His decision to override William Fitzroger's summons to the Holy Land by his order was therefore certainly not due to an ignorance of the seriousness of the crusader position there. Edward must have had a very pressing reason for ordering the prior to return to Ireland immediately, and there can be little doubt that this was the rebellion in Wicklow that had still not been suppressed.

Hugh Revel, who summoned Fitzroger to the East and wrote to Edward I about the situation there, was one of the most autocratic masters of the Hospitallers in the Middle Ages. In 1262 a chapter general of the order, convened by Revel, decreed that if any Hospitaller brother in Europe failed to comply with its orders he would be compelled to travel to the East and would lose his habit. According to a leading modern authority on the Hospitallers, 'this made it virtually impossible to question a magisterial order'.[15] It also provides a context for William Fitzroger's statement, contained in the text of Edward I's letter, that he 'could not disobey this summons or break … oaths and promises of obedience'. It is interesting, moreover, that in 1283 another chapter general of the order laid down that if a prior was recalled to the central convent but detained by a prince he would have to pay a fine and the master could replace him if he wished. The situation envisaged in this statute is strikingly similar to the quarrel that arose between Edward I and William Fitzroger in 1275. Even if not directly connected, it represents a recognition that there was potential tension within the order's ranks between devotion to the cross and other non-crusading obligations.

In 1275 Edward I insisted that William Fitzroger abandon his planned journey to the East and return 'for the good of the crown and the entire land of Ireland'. Although Fitzroger must have had serious misgivings about this, and perhaps also feared that he might lose his priorship as a result, he obeyed and the king got his way. Fitzroger never went to the East and his career as a royal servant continued notwithstanding his crusader commitments. Certainly it cannot be said that his intention to go to the Holy Land instead of returning to Ireland in 1275 was motivated by a wish to wage war on Muslims in the East rather than on fellow Christians at home, for he led royal armies against the Irish both before and after 1275, evidently without demur. In the summer of 1285, for example, he was making preparations for another campaign against the king's enemies in Connacht, at which time he also held the position of *locum tenens* for the justiciar of Ireland.[16] Fitzroger's successors as priors of the order of St John of Jerusalem in Ireland continued to fight against the enemies of the king. In 1302 Prior William de Ros was paid to levy troops in Leinster 'for the preservation of the king's peace'. In 1318 Prior Roger Outlawe and his brother knights were compensated for losses incurred while in the service of the king during the Bruce invasion of Ireland. In 1360 an entry in the close roll of Edward III noted that the Hospitallers in Ireland 'hold there a good position for the repulse of the king's enemies daily warring upon his liege people'.[17] Not one of these wars was remotely connected with the crusades.

William Fitzroger's dilemma thus originated from the dual obligations he owed within the respective hierarchies of the royal administration and his crusading order. Since he did not hold any office in the lordship of Ireland in 1275, he must have considered himself answerable first and foremost to his institutional superior, Hugh Revel, master of the Hospitallers, although Edward I chose to see it differently. It is worth noting that, although Fitzroger's successors were also faithful servants of the crown, conflicting loyalties between royal service and crusading came to the surface in Ireland again in later years. In 1400 Henry IV forbade Prior Peter Holt to leave Ireland and travel to the East without a royal licence; his brother Hospitallers were subjected to the same ban and even prevented from sending money overseas.[18] The Hospitallers in Ireland were, in fact, always far more active as royal servants than as crusaders. It is surprising and rather ironic that the professional crusading forces raised in Ireland in the thirteenth and fourteenth centuries are remembered for fighting not against the Saracens but against the Irish.

The Wife's Tale

GILLIAN KENNY

In February 1348 a woman died in Dublin. She was probably middle-aged, she was a mother, she had been a wife and her death was just one of many that were to occur in that terrible year as the Black Death swept across Ireland. She left behind children and close friends who doubtless mourned her loss. Some of them may have died soon after her, succumbing to the plague as the death toll mounted. We know of this woman because, remarkably, a copy was made of her will and has been preserved in Trinity College. Her name was Giliana de Moenis and she and her family lived and died in the bustling medieval metropolis that was fourteenth-century Dublin.[1]

Medieval Dublin, with its overwhelming smells, vivid colours and busy, cramped streets, was the home town of the de Moenis/Moenes family by the mid-fourteenth century. They were originally from England and derived their surname from Moen in Hampshire. William de Moenes first came to Ireland in 1279 and served as an important official in the colonial administration. He probably died sometime around 1325. The family held extensive lands in Rathmines, a settlement south of the medieval city, and during the fourteenth century members of the family regularly attained the position of mayor of Dublin. Thus, Giliana was born into a well-off, well-connected and politically powerful family. In this tale I hope to show you what life was like for a townswoman in fourteenth-century Dublin by looking at what we know of Giliana de Moenis through the prism of her will and by describing the conditions of life at that time.

First of all, to set the scene, let us look at the physical living conditions that Giliana would have had to contend with living in Dublin. Like all medieval towns, Dublin was pretty unsanitary by modern standards. Every householder was supposed to clean the street in front of his or her house but the almost eternal complaints from city authorities suggest that many inhabitants of the city did not do so on a regular basis. From time to time people were fined for leaving nuisances such as piles of dung outside their houses. Problems concerning the keeping of animals were ongoing. The city council legislated against unpenned pigs, for example, that roamed the city, sometimes disturbing newly buried bodies in graveyards as they rooted around for food. Many streets would have been rank with the smell of human and animal effluent and, like all medieval towns, the consequences of the cramped conditions meant that contagious diseases were rife. Medieval Dubliners did not understand the mechanisms by which cleanliness was a protection from illness, but housewives (like Giliana) did attempt to keep up their own standards of hygiene. Medieval wives were concerned with keeping their houses as clean as they could. They (or their servants in some cases) scrubbed floors, washed clothes and hung them out to dry on surrounding hedges, scraped food from plates and cleaned them, put fresh rushes down and beat beds to try to disperse some of the lice and fleas. People did the best they could with the limited amount of knowledge they had.

Of course not all wives were as fussy as our Dublin housewife, but most did try because in the Middle Ages foul-smelling homes had connotations of sinfulness, corruption and decay. Cleanliness was therefore an important aspect of a respectable person's identity. It was, after all, considered to be next to godliness. This link also required people to pay attention to their personal appearance. Mothers would bathe their babies and wrap them in linen, which was ideally sweetened with rose petals ground with salt, on a regular basis. Adults, it is true, did not often bathe fully – it was time-consuming to heat the water – but they did wash regularly. A woman like Giliana would also ensure that her clothes were clean and would have paid particular attention to her wimple, or headpiece, the spotless sign of a respectable married woman. She might also, as a well-off member of Dublin society, have used perfume, perhaps one made from musk, lavender or rosewater. She may literally have smelled of roses as she went about her daily business in Dublin. Thus, even though fourteenth-century Dubliners were not quite up to our modern levels of hygiene, they were in fact strict about maintaining certain standards.[2]

These standards were also strictly adhered to in the case of manners and politeness. Medieval Dublin was doubtless fairly dirty, violent and uncouth at times but its inhabitants would have had high standards of politeness. Behaving appropriately was very important to medieval people, especially in the company of their betters. Since the Moenis family was near the top of the social ladder in Dublin, Giliana may have been socially intimidated only by visiting aristocracy. Television and films often portray medieval meals as consisting of people gnawing on joints of meat and then hurling bones around the hall. This is not an accurate representation of how Giliana and her friends and family would have eaten. Rules of etiquette were especially important when it came to eating socially. In a medieval house, such as the well-heeled one that Giliana ran, everyone washed their hands before every meal and cut their bread rather than breaking it up with their hands. Rules such as not leaning on the table were also followed during this period and speaking with your mouth full or talking to anyone when they were drinking were both frowned upon. Women in particular were expected to behave in a seemly manner. For example, it was considered uncouth for women to swear and drunkenness in women was considered shocking. Drunkenness was also associated with licentiousness: hence less respectable women, such as tavern keepers, often had poor reputations. A woman such as Giliana was careful to guard her behaviour.

A well-run medieval household like Giliana's was dependent on its staff and much of this staff was made up of women. Though roles such as domestic service were badly paid and difficult, they provided women with economic opportunities not available in the countryside. They also provided upper-class women with opportunities to assemble a close-knit group of female servants with whom they often became quite intimate. In Giliana's will she specifically named and singled out one such female servant for a bequest; she gave Isabella Feld 18*d.* in respect of her service. Therefore, although life in Dublin presented challenges with disease, dirt and sometimes difficult living conditions, it also provided the chance for economic betterment for poorer women who could enter service and thus earn their own pay and participate in mutually beneficial female social networks with their (female) employers. The wife of the medieval house was in charge of organizing servants and she would have been a powerful female nexus around which female servants gathered and looked to benefit from.

As a young girl, wife, mother and eventually widow, Giliana's Dublin was also a place where you could have fun. Towns were centres of not only economic opportunity but also entertainment. In her house, Giliana may have hosted dances and, as a medieval Dubliner, she would also have seen plays performed. The most common sorts were the miracle plays and mystery plays that were performed on feast days in the large towns of Ireland, as they were in towns across Europe. At Christmas she would have enjoyed mummers' performances where masks were used, as were disguises. Perhaps Giliana played dice with friends and family on long winter evenings or 'cross and pile', which was the medieval name for heads and tails played with coins. She may also have played chess, an early form of backgammon or draughts.

Entertainment could lighten what might often be a difficult life of privation for some people. Not all townswomen were relatively well-off like Giliana. Indeed, most townswomen earned their living through a variety of activities, including labouring, brewing, baking, landholding (that is, income from rents), tavern-keeping, prostitution and craftwork (pl. 8). Medieval townswomen generally tried to make money through the production of alcohol (as in ale) or foodstuffs such as the pies that they sold either from their houses or from booths or stalls. In 1455 the regulation of all ale measures was addressed exclusively to female brewers in Dublin. They were forbidden to adulterate the product by brewing with straw and, if any woman was found guilty of selling inferior ale, she was to be fined first and then suspended if she kept offending.

The working women of Dublin appear to have been largely relegated to the least remunerated class of labour. A record of the accounts of the

Augustinian house of the Holy Trinity at Christ Church showcases the characteristically low wages given to women in the fourteenth and fifteenth centuries. The labouring wage paid to women was 1/2*d.* a day, whereas the normal wage for their male equivalent was 1*d.* a day. At 50 per cent of male wages, the pay for these women compared unfavourably with that of their contemporaries in Bristol or Yorkshire, for example, where the differential between male and female rates of pay was an average of 75 per cent and 71 per cent respectively. Women may also have occupied a subsidiary roll in the family business and have been excluded from some aspects of their husband's trade. For example, in 1451 the wives of butchers and fishermen were expressly forbidden to sell meat and fish, and this was reiterated in 1456–7. By 1464–5, however, the city council relented and there was no active opposition to women selling fish. Giliana may herself have occasionally helped out her husband in his daily tasks, though we do not know what his occupation was.

From the fact that her husband is not mentioned in her will, it is plausible that he predeceased her and she lived as a widow for some time before her own death. We do not know how long he had been dead but it is possible to speculate that Giliana, with her social and economic advantages, may not have felt either the need or the inclination to remarry (pl. 10). As an economically independent widow, the law enabled her to conduct business much as a man could. She could enter into contracts, buy and sell goods and lands and live a busy life answerable to no one. Records of grants of unspecified lands from widows are relatively plentiful in town records, where widows were often a noticeable part of the workforce and sometimes also employers. Wealthier widows were also expected to play their part in town defences. The records of Dublin's city council contain notices that 'widows with property shall contribute towards the watch and ward proportionately with their neighbours'. The council also provided for the intervention of the mayor to settle property claims between widows and heirs. Giliana lived in a society in which women could engage productively in business and, if they were able, flourish as widows. As a widow from a prominent and powerful family, her experiences were not identical to those of other, less wealthy, women. Nevertheless, her will serves as a fascinating window into the details of one medieval woman's life.

Apart from these more mundane events and circumstances in Giliana's life in medieval Dublin, she must also have witnessed some remarkable events in the city's history. Giliana was most likely middle-aged at the time of her death in 1348. We know this because many of her bequests to her daughters varied in size and were perhaps reflective of the fact that some were married and thus provided for and others were not. If she was in the 35–50 age-range (remember that marriage was allowed at 12 for girls) then she would have been witness to some remarkable events in Irish history. The early fourteenth century was a particularly tumultuous time for the English colony in Ireland. She may, for example, have remembered the Scottish attack on Dublin. In 1317, Dublin was threatened by a Scottish army. Following their victory at Bannockburn in 1314, the Scots, led by Edward Bruce, invaded Ireland. Desperate efforts were made to repair the walls around Dublin, which were in a constant state of disrepair, while the only bridge over the Liffey was destroyed to prevent the Scots from using it. Finally, the authorities set fire to the western suburbs of Dublin (in case they provided cover for an advancing army). Unfortunately, the fire got out of hand and destroyed far more buildings than was intended. All of these preparations and skirmishes occurred while Dublin was still suffering the ramifications of the terrible European famine of 1315. Conditions within the city at this time would thus have been particularly dire. As a wealthy child, however, Giliana may have been shielded from the worst consequences of these events. One of the major catastrophes of the fourteenth century that she missed was the arrival of the Black Death in Ireland in July 1348, for her will was made in the February of that year, suggesting she was very ill months before the plague hit and most likely died before summer. Thus, when we read Giliana's will, her anxiety to provide for her loved ones is a poignant reminder that many of these friends and relatives must have followed her to the grave before the year was out.

The plague, known as the Black Death, was the greatest disaster to hit medieval Europe and Dublin was not exempted from its horrors. It is difficult to imagine the levels of suffering that were endured in such a cramped, closely interwoven and interrelated society in which everyone knew everyone else. It is hard for us, so many years later, to comprehend the scale of the tragedy. In 1348, as Giliana lay dying and composing herself to meet her god, she may be considered fortunate that she died before she could witness the misery that the plague would inflict on her home town and on those she loved, so soon after she passed away.

She made her will on her deathbed as most medieval people did. Wills in the Middle Ages consisted essentially of two parts – bequests for the good of the soul and arrangements for the descent of secular property, which could be both land and chattels. The wills made by widows in late medieval Ireland followed this format. Usually, a will began by bequeathing the soul to God, then the place of burial was specified and arrangements for the funeral were made, including the masses that were to be said for the testator. What followed was a list of legacies and bequests to loved ones and friends as well as to parish churches and religious houses. Executors and witnesses were also named to ensure proper adherence to the testator's wishes. Widows generally had chattels to dispose of from the pre- and post-marital home, even though the heir had first choice of all chattels. There were no restraints on how a widow distributed those chattels, which might have included jewellery, plate, weapons and books. Widows could also dispose of lands they might have acquired or inherited as they chose.

Unusually, Giliana's will centred on bequests of clothes and goods to other women – family, friends and servants. As I have mentioned, she gave 18*d.* to Isabella Feld 'for her service'. She also granted a tunic to Agnes Horister. Women's clothing at that time was still quite simple in construction, but could be embroidered, dyed, decorated or made from luxury fabrics, depending on price. The kirtle or gown was worn over a shift and under a tunic like the one that Giliana gifted to Agnes. Perhaps it was a favourite tunic of Agnes'. There is no information about Agnes' relationship to Giliana in the will, but given that she was remembered with this personal bequest of clothing, she may have been a close friend. One woman in particular received a large number of gifts from Giliana. She was named as

Isabella, the daughter of William son of Richard, who was, presumably, unmarried and may have been Giliana's grand-niece. She received a bed worth half a mark, three napkins, three towels, a silver cup worth half a mark, a mazer cup worth 20*d.* and a girdle worth half a mark. Since Isabella seems to have been unmarried, these items may have been intended as the foundation for a dowry. Granting a relative a dowry and a means to marry was considered a great act of charity during the Middle Ages. The gifts also indicated Giliana's economic position. The inclusion of a mazer cup, for example, is interesting. This was a vessel made usually from maple wood and designed for drinking the wines of Burgundy and Toulouse since these lost their bouquet when drunk from a metal cup. Giliana, it seems, was used to the finer things in life.

Additionally, her will paid close attention to the needs of her family, as well as to more public acts of charity. She left 12*d.* to her daughter Joan, as well as a dress and a coverlet with two linen cloths. Two other daughters and what may have been a step-daughter received her house opposite the church of St Michael on High Street in Dublin. It was situated at the corner of Christ Church Lane, immediately opposite the western end of the cathedral, where the former Synod Hall now stands (see St Michael's, near no. 47 on Speed's 1610 map of Dublin, p. ii above). Another daughter received a dress and Giliana's sister was granted an overtunic and a bed. Beds, in the Middle Ages, were prized possessions and the fact that she bequeathed two beds also indicates the extent of Giliana's wealth. Beds and bedding were so valuable and highly prized that they were not passed casually down the generations, and it is not unusual to find them mentioned in wills. A well-to-do but middling family might have one featherbed and a feather bolster to pass on, while some of the wealthiest people could leave their descendants several beds with complete sets of expensive hangings and fine bedding. Even woollen mattresses were important enough to be passed on as a bequest in some families. Giliana's bequest of beds would presumably have been very much appreciated by those relatives she favoured.

Although the number of bequests to women was unusual, one aspect of Giliana's will was more traditional. It began with a bequest for the good of her soul and a request concerning where she might be buried. She asked that she be buried in the cemetery of the Fratres in Dublin. This is the Hospital of St John the Baptist, which was run by the Fratres Cruciferi. This was obviously a favoured institution, since she also put aside 5s. 6d. for feeding the infirm of St John's. Like Giliana, medieval townspeople were, for the most part, conventionally religious; many members of urban families were among the parish priests or locally based friars, monks or nuns. But they were also worldly. Sometimes their donations or bequests to religious houses were motivated by a bad conscience over un-Christian business practices; provisions for charitable bequests were therefore occasionally very elaborate. The church was a valued part of Dublin life. Giliana's bequest to the Hospital of St John the Baptist displays the usual concerns of medieval female piety – those of hospitality, devotion and charity. Her charitable impulse was probably also a practical attempt to alleviate some of the ills visible around the area in which she lived. The church itself was very active in promoting the use of wills as a way to provide relief, through the provision of charity, for the testator's soul. Additionally, church courts rather than civil ones dealt with probate and any disputes concerning wills in late medieval Ireland and these donations to the church might assist one's heirs if their rights to bequests were challenged.

Widows possessed the freedom to make unsupervised grants to the church, but donations of dower or jointure lands were only for the lifetime of the widow unless the heir's consent was sought and obtained for a permanent alienation. Lands that widows had inherited were theirs to donate. The benefits to be accrued from such grants were not measured purely in monetary terms. It must have been a source of great comfort to many widows that such grants meant years of masses and prayers said for the benefit of their own or their loved ones' eternal souls. Giliana's grant of money was made to pay for masses that would ease her soul out of purgatory and into heaven. Religious concerns and anxiety about the afterlife were very important to medieval Dubliners and such bequests were a necessary comfort as they faced death.

Giliana's life as a medieval Dubliner was one that, like that of the majority of medieval women, focused on family. This is reflected in her will – the stark legal language not completely serving to hide the lifetime of love and affection for her sister, friends, servants and daughters. Her life was one that displays the importance to medieval women of close female friendships. She honoured them in her last thoughts. She was a widow whose wealth and membership in a powerful family probably enabled her to stay that way by choice until her death. As an independent widow in fourteenth-century Dublin she had greater freedom than a married woman to act as she chose. She could make donations to the church, act as a patron, pursue her debtors and generally dispose of her affairs as she liked. This was the course that Giliana took and the scant details of her life (as evidenced in her will) give us a brief but enlightening look into the life and concerns of a well-to-do widow in late medieval Dublin.

The Mason's Tale

MICHAEL O'NEILL

John More, mason, was an important figure in the maintenance of medieval Dublin. He was the mason at Dublin Castle in 1372 and was instrumental in the repair of the great bridge of Dublin in 1385–6. These landmarks of the city are visible on the scale model of Dublin *c*.1500, exhibited in Dublinia and photographed and published in the *Irish Historic Towns Atlas* of Dublin (pl. 11). This model dramatically illustrates three of the most important aspects of the city. Firstly, it was the centre of the administration of the colony, housed in Dublin Castle (A on pl. 11); secondly, it was a focus of religious life, as shown by its two cathedrals and many monastic foundations (B on pl. 11); and finally it was at the heart of a massive trade network based around the river and bridge crossing (C on pl. 11). More, as a master mason in Dublin in the later fourteenth century, was responsible for maintaining and rebuilding infrastructures relating to two if not three of these vital roles of the city in its hinterland.

We know little about More's education, family and early life but we can extrapolate something about his education and training from what we know about medieval masons more generally. John Harvey, the architectural historian, has provided a good summary of the education and background of a typical medieval master mason:

> Much confusion still exists in the minds of many readers as to the methods by which the remarkable buildings of the Middle Ages were designed and, in particular, as to who were the designers. It has to be repeated that most of the really great architects in the years between AD1050 and 1550 where men who, *besides any other educa-*

tion they might receive, underwent a full training as stonemasons or carpenters – sometimes in both crafts. Over and above merely manual skill they went on to learn by rote **geometrical secrets of two kinds**; on the one hand these were **methods of manipulating a straightedge or square and a pair of compasses** so as to produce a right angle; **the repeated proportion of the diagonal to the side of a square**; the '**Golden Cut**' proportion infinitely repeating itself, and the like. Secondly, the secrets concerned **structural stability and comprised memorized proportions of depth and bulk of foundations in relation to the width and height of the building proposed**, with safety factors allowing for wind-pressure and the thrusts of vaults and roofs and the needed buttresses ... There could not have been 'amateur architects' in the period down to 1500 or later, and the often repeated statements that the monks and the clergy were 'architects' are necessarily false.[1]

If, as Harvey suggests, men like More required many years of speciality training, he may have been an English master mason trained in England before coming over to Ireland. His arrival in Dublin coincided with the increase in building activity of all types – bridges, castles, smaller castles or tower houses, parish churches, friaries and monasteries – that started in the later fourteenth century after a considerable hiatus in the middle decades as a result of the Bruce wars and the Black Death. More, then, may have been one of several English master masons who arrived in Ireland to participate in the beginning of the late medieval building boom.

The earliest mention of John More, mason, in Dublin dates to 30 April 1372, when he was described as a *clericus operacionum*, 'clerk of works', and was granted £20 for work on Dublin Castle and projects elsewhere in Leinster. We have no indication of what buildings or repairs More supervised as clerk of works at Dublin Castle from either documentary or archaeological sources. One of the reasons that so little evidence survives is the extent to which Dublin Castle was remodelled in the course of the eighteenth and nineteenth centuries, as can be seen from an isometric reconstruction of the castle in the medieval period produced by Ann Lynch and Conleth Manning. Even if our documentary sources told us something about the work on the castle that More supervised, the likelihood of it surviving to the present day in any form is therefore quite remote (fig. 10.1).

More also worked elsewhere in the colony and can be found in 1381 repairing Carlow Castle.[2] The £20 paid to More for his work on Carlow Castle pales into insignificance when compared with expenditures some twenty years earlier. A notable high point in the castle's history was in 1361 when Lionel, the son of King Edward III, then duke of Clarence and justiciar of Ireland, removed the exchequer from Dublin to Carlow. In doing so, he spent £500 in strengthening the fortifications there. In spite of this, the exchequer was later removed back to Dublin owing to the increasingly unstable nature of the area around Carlow. The small fee paid suggests that the modifications More made to Carlow Castle were minor, just like those he made to Dublin Castle ten years previously.

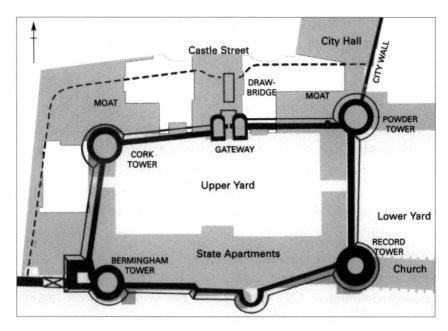

10.1 Plan of Dublin Castle (image courtesy of Conleth Manning and Wordwell).

We have rather more documentary and visual evidence surviving regarding the works that More performed on the great bridge of Dublin. On 1 March 1386, he and Nicholas Mason were ordered to take masons to repair the great bridge of Dublin, which was located near modern-day Bridge Street.[3] The 'taking of masons' in order to repair the bridge almost certainly refers to a common practice of pressing masons into service. This means that the masons were given no choice in the matter, but forcibly employed on large-scale building projects. In the castle-building campaigns of Edward I in Wales in the late thirteenth century, whole counties of masons were pressed to build castles.

A second document, a grant of Richard II dating to 1386, provides additional information regarding the bridge works. This grant gave permission for a ferry to replace the damaged bridge and for the operator to charge tolls or tariffs that would be applied towards the cost of repairing the bridge. It also provides information regarding the nature of animal farming and trade associated with the medieval city:

> great inconvenience and damage have been caused to the citizens of Dublin, and other liege subjects, by the fall and the breaking down of the great bridge of that city. To aid towards its repair, the king, by the advice of Philip de Courtenay, his lieutenant in Ireland, and his council there, grants to the mayor, bailiffs and citizens during the ensuing four years, the city ferry over the Liffey, with permission to take the following tolls: of every man and woman one farthing; of every ox, cow, horse, mare and horse-load valued at twelve pence, also of every ox carcass, one halfpenny; of every load of less value, and of every pig, sheep, ox carcass thereof, one farthing; of all other goods ferried, a reasonable toll, in proportion to quality and value, according to the discretion of the mayor and bailiffs. The issues and receipts of the ferry-tolls and customs, beyond the reasonable outlay, are to be applied towards the repair and construction of the bridge, under the supervision of the Abbot of the House of the Blessed Virgin Mary, near Dublin, Edmund Berle, Nicholas Sergeant,

Robert Burnell, Nicholas Howth, John Bermyngham and James Maureward; annual accounts are to be rendered at the king's exchequer in Ireland.[4]

Remarkably, the medieval great bridge of Dublin survived into the early nineteenth century and is captured pictorially in James Malton's 'View of the Four Courts' in 1799 (pl. 12). Malton's view looks west and is taken from Ormond Bridge. In the middle distance, he captured the four-bay humpbacked bridge and the cutwaters extending up onto the bridge parapet. The south-side arrises reflect the sunlight mirror-like, while the neo-classical Four Courts on the north bank are bathed in light. There is a record of additional repairs done to this bridge in 1428, which stated that

> the Dominican friars erected with the assistance of their benefactors the old bridge, and to repay them, a lay brother of the order, one of the common council of the city, received at the bridge a penny (*denarius*) for every carriage, horse and beast of burthen passing over it.[5]

Accordingly, there is some question as to whether the bridge depicted by Malton – a bridge that survived until it was replaced in 1816 and renamed Whitworth Bridge – was that built by More or was the work of a later unnamed architect of the 1420s. It is surely more romantic to suggest that the bridge structure captured by Malton is that rebuilt by More, but there is no way to be certain.

While these documentary sources demonstrate that More completed some works on both Dublin Castle and the great bridge, it is possible that he was also partially responsible for repairs done to St Patrick's Cathedral in 1370. The fact that More is documented as being in Dublin in 1372 for repairs to Dublin Castle suggested to the architectural historian John Harvey that More was also the supervising architect at St Patrick's Cathedral around 1370 when the north-western tower, called Minot's tower, was rebuilt. In April 1362 'John the sexton' was accused of being responsible for a fire in the cathedral and Archbishop Minot sent a petition to the pope in 1363 'for relaxation for seven years … of enjoined penance to those who lend a helping hand to the repair of the church of St Patrick, Dublin, which by negligence and fire has so greatly suffered that the tower and bells are destroyed'. Sir James Ware related that Minot both repaired the part of St Patrick's church that had been destroyed by the accidental fire and built a very high steeple of hewn stone about the year 1370. After these efforts, Minot took up the custom of using the device of a bishop holding a steeple in his hand in his official seal. In the ancient registry of St Patrick's Church, commencing 1367 and formerly in the custody of Dean Culme, there is evidence that many of the construction workers were not professionals or even volunteers, but were pressed into service, like those who were forced to help in the repairs on the great bridge. The registry noted:

> After the burning of St Patrick's Church, sixty straggling and idle fellows were taken up and obliged to assist in repairing the church and building the steeple; who when their work was over, returned to their old trade of begging; but were banished out of the diocese in 1376 by Robert de Wikeford, successor to this prelate. Their names are inserted in the register at large.[6]

Were these simply workmen or might they have been a band of itinerant masons who were afterwards seemingly banished not only from the city, but also from the diocese of Dublin by a subsequent prelate? Either way it is clear that they did not volunteer for the positions.

If he did indeed work on St Patrick's, then More was responsible for infrastructure relating to three of the most important aspects of life in the medieval city: the administration of the city (Dublin Castle), trade and transport (the great bridge) and the religious well-being of the community (St Patrick's Cathedral). While we do not know much about the man himself, More's work was vital to the inhabitants of medieval Dublin and he may have left more of himself in the city than we think. A discursive and lavishly illustrated study of the medieval master mason is provided by

Nicola Coldstream in *Medieval craftsmen, masons and sculptors*. In this work, Coldstream provides depictions of master masons on canvas and in manuscript illustrations and a photograph of the self-portrait bust of Peter Parler, architect of Prague Cathedral, placed high in the choir. More than one mason was keen to represent himself in his work, and there is also a bust at the west end of the north nave triforium of Wells Cathedral that is thought to depict the master mason Adam Lock, who died in 1229. There is a similar late fourteenth-century head bust in the nave of St Patrick's Cathedral in Dublin, wearing what appears to be a mason's cap. It may seem fanciful, but could this be the face of John More, our master mason of the late fourteenth century (fig. 10.2)?

10.2 Mason's head from St Patrick's Cathedral (© Edwin Rae Collection, TRIARC, Irish Art Research Centre).

The Notary's Tale

༶ঔৡৣ༶

CAOIMHE WHELAN

James Yonge was a legal practitioner, a notary by occupation, who provided legal services for the people of Dublin. His considerable literary abilities drew him into higher circles, where he became a minor player in the power-struggles that dominated the political landscape of fifteenth-century Ireland. His status as one of the few known literary figures in Hiberno-Middle English (the dialect of English spoken in medieval Ireland) adds to his intriguing history. The tale of James Yonge gives us a striking impression of the life and career of one professional fifteenth-century Dubliner.

There are some traces of prominent members of the Yonge family before and after James. Some of the Yonges of Dublin were quite successful, and there were numerous merchants, churchmen and government officials in the extended family during the Middle Ages. It is difficult to be certain about some of the facts of James' life, but Theresa O'Byrne has identified Edmund Yonge, who died in 1418, as his father. James was probably born *c*.1375–80. In 1415, towards the end of his life, Edmund was living, possibly with his second wife Amice, in a house facing Merchant's Quay in the parish of St Audoen (see no. 9 on Speed's map above, p. ii). The house had a narrow covered portico passage that led onto Cook Street, while a small stream called Colman's brook (now underground) flowed on the east of the house and then traversed the back garden (see no. 28 on p. ii). Yonge may have lived in this house for some time, or at least have been a frequent visitor.

O'Byrne suggests that James Yonge was destined for a career as a member of the minor clergy, and possibly received a clerical education. He never became a cleric, however, and it appears that he married some time before 1406, which would have prevented ecclesiastical advancement. Yonge instead embarked on a secular career and probably trained as a clerk under the bearer of the seal of the provostship of Dublin (pl. 13). The clerk who held this position in the Dublin municipal administration had responsibility for the seal used to authenticate documents when a grantor's seal was not well known and it was sometimes used to authentic outcomes of arbitration in property disputes. Thus, the seal provided the grantee security and imbued the transaction with legal authority. Yonge seems to have graduated to become a bearer of the seal of the provostship and held that office for most of his working life; his hand is evident on some of the documents bearing the seal from the early to mid-fifteenth century. Of course, Yonge was also a notary, a legal functionary who specialized in witnessing, drafting and recording legal contracts (administrative or ecclesiastical) – sales, charters, wills and the like, and on occasion he acted as an attorney in property transactions (pl. 14). The low remuneration awarded to notaries probably incentivized participation in other areas. There are numerous examples of skilled professionals such as notaries engaged in literary commissions in both Ireland and England in this period: Geoffrey Chaucer, often called the 'father of English literature' (*c.*1343–1400), was involved in official business for the crown, while Thomas Hoccleve (*c.*1368–1426), the author of the *Regiment for princes* dedicated to King Henry V of England (a text that Yonge attempted to emulate), was a privy seal clerk in London. With their literary skills acquired and honed in the course of their primary jobs, these professionals were able to supplement their income by acting as scribes for hire and earn extra money. In one of the literary commissions that Yonge undertook in 1411, he gave a description of himself that underlined this bipartite identity:

ego Iacobus Yonge, notarius Imperialis, civium & scriptorum minimus civitatis Dublinensis predicte, huius memorialis compilator indignus coram Deo ...

I, James Yonge, imperial notary and least of the citizens and writers of the aforesaid city of Dublin, the unworthy compiler of this history before God ...[1]

This portrayal demonstrates his occupation as a professional notary and his involvement in the creation of literary works. He described himself as *notarius imperialis* – an imperial notary – which placed him at the centre of the administration of law in the English colony in Ireland, since it was through people like James Yonge that the machinery of everyday law and contracts functioned efficiently. Even so, the description also contained a humility *topos* denoting his place in medieval Dublin society – he is 'the least of the citizens and writers' and 'the unworthy compiler' of this text. Of course, this self-effacing representation was not an accurate reflection of his literary ability (which was great), but a common refrain of a writer seeking to portray himself as humble.

Yonge's professional work was not all mundane and unremarkable; he had a fruitful relationship with one of the most powerful men in Ireland in this period, James Butler, fourth earl of Ormond, who twice held the office of lieutenant of Ireland. The earl appointed him to the office of second engrosser of the Irish exchequer in 1420 and also directly employed him to undertake legal matters relating to the earl's business interests in 1428 and 1429 (when he was involved in writing grants, quit-claims and deeds of attorney). Nevertheless, perhaps his most interesting connection with Ormond came in the form of a commissioned text, the *Governance of prynces*, a translation undertaken in 1422 in which Yonge included a passage on what to look for when employing a notary. The original text, addressed to Alexander the Great, did not mention notaries, but Yonge altered the passage that referred to 'private secretaries' and instead wrote about what he considered to be a much more important job; that of the 'notary'.

Of Notaries. *Capitulum* Lm.
Alexandyr, to chese the be-houeth, to writte thy Pryuyteis and priuey workys, wyse men of Parfite eloquence, and of good mynde. For that is a tokyn of a grete lorde, and a stronge argument to Shewe the heynesse of thy myght, and the Sotilte of thy knowleche.[2]

Alexander, it is necessary to choose, to write your valuable and private works, wise men of perfect eloquence, and of good mind.

For that is a token of a great lord, and a strong argument to show the highness of your might, and the subtlety of your knowledge.[3]

Yonge went on to explain that a good notary should:

be of good feyth hit nedyth know thy wille in al thynges, and that he wyllyth thy profite and honoure afor al thynges; he sholde be curteyse and Parceuynge in his dedis, And tha no man entyr in sygh of thy Preveyteis of wrytynges.[4]

be of good faith, he needs to know your will in all things, and that he desires your profit and honour before all things; he should be courteous and perceptive in his deeds, and [ensure] that no man enter in sight of your valuable writings.

Yonge finally reached what for him was the most important part, when he warned his patron:

And yf thou mayste fynde hym Suche, Pay hym well for his Service, so that he hym holde apayed to do the bettyr.[5]

And if you find such as him, pay him well for his service, so that he is obliged to improve.

Although Yonge's original manuscript does not survive, a contemporary copy of the text is found in the Bodleian Library in Oxford (Rawlinson B490) and it illustrates medieval spelling in English in a fifteenth-century Irish dialect. Medieval spelling was not standardized so authors wrote phonetically, which means that spelling can provide clues as to how dialects sounded; amazingly, this gives us a glimpse of the Irish dialect of the mid-1400s. Before they could put words on a page, however, the notary had to master the physical art of writing – not a common skill in the Middle Ages. As part of their job, notaries were often called on to witness contracts, take notes and later produce an official record. A French image from an early fifteenth-century manuscript in the British Library (Royal 19 C XI) depicts a scribe with the tools of his trade (pl. 15). The scribe is depicted with a quill perched behind his ear, a portable ink well, and a pen-holder hanging from his waist, while he holds a large crescent-shaped knife called a *lunarium* or *lunellum* (called after the Latin for moon, which often appears in a crescent shape) in his hand to remove hairs on parchment. By the fifteenth century, most scribes – and certainly notaries – would not have had to prepare their own parchment, since it could be purchased from shops that sold it in various forms, shapes and sizes, which the scribe could select according to his purpose.

Although notaries could probably buy writing implements, they had to prepare and maintain their quills. Generally, a scribe wrote with his or her right hand, with the result that pens were often made from feathers taken from the left-wing of a bird in order to utilize the natural curve. The feathers were cut back – at least on the underside – to make the quill easier to hold and use, rendering it closer in looks to our modern pen. The nib of the quill had to be pared back before it could be used, and for long documents it would have had to be sharpened throughout the writing project with a knife. The knife was central to the process of writing. While they wrote, scribes normally held a quill in one hand and a knife in the other; the knife could be used to sharpen the pen when necessary – the origin of our term 'pen-knife'. But the knife was also pivotal to the writing process in other ways – it was used to hold the page steady (to prevent inky fingerprints from staining the page) and for wiping or scratching mistakes away. Since the quill was a dip pen, scribes held it straighter than modern pens, topping up their ink from a bottle standing close by and often using slanted desks to aid the flow of ink. If they were copying a document, weights were often hung over the manuscript to keep the folios of the copy-text open and steady. James Yonge would have been familiar with all of these skills and techniques and it would not have been difficult to adapt his experience in writing legal documents to copy and write other, non-legal texts.

All notaries had their own notarial sign – *signum manuale* – which they drew at the end of their document to indicate their authorship. Some of the documents in Yonge's hand survive and his sign is also known: it is evident, for example, on a manuscript in the Royal Irish Academy (RIA 12S22–31, no. 343) (fig. 11.1). A notary's work could be quite varied; one document in Latin from 1405 shows James Yonge's work in relation to a case of unlawful imprisonment:

> James Yonge, clerk, notary public, certifies that on the 16th March, 1405, in the hall of the inn of John Gardener, citizen of Dublin, in Cow Lane, Parish of St Audoen, John Lytill, citizen, stated that he had been arrested at the suit of Robert Burnell [a former mayor of Dublin] & lodged in prison because he refused to sign and seal certain writings & documents at the will of the said Robert, & for no other cause.[6]

11.1 James Yonge's *signum manuale* from RIA MS 12 S 22–31, no. 343, 12 December 1432 (by permission of the Royal Irish Academy © RIA).

Lytill was a wealthy man in the parish of St John the Evangelist (Bothe Street; near no. 35 on Speed's map above, p. ii) and Lytill and Yonge often appear together in the records over a thirty-year period. They certainly appear to have had a good working relationship and were most likely friends. But Lytill was not the only Dubliner who employed Yonge. A few years after this document, in November 1411, Yonge was involved in a property transaction:

> James [*Yonge*], clerk, notary public, certifies that on the 28th Nov. 1411 in the mansion house of Simon Dodenale, merchant [a neighbour of Yonge's father], on 'the Key' [the south side] of Dublin, the said Simon having granted to John Stafford & John Ingoll, chaplains, three houses and three gardens in 'Oxemaneston' [on the north side of the river], Johanna, wife of the said Simon, swore that she had no claim to dower upon the said property.[7]

In the same year, we catch sight of James Yonge, this time not engaged in legal matters, but rather producing a literary text for a Hungarian nobleman, Lawrence Rathold of Pászthó in northern Hungary, who came to Ireland in 1411 as a pilgrim to visit St Patrick's purgatory at Lough Derg in Co. Donegal. Yonge tells us that it was the citizens of Dublin – captivated by the Hungarian knight's story – who persuaded Rathold to have his account written down. The Latin account of the trip that Yonge produced is somewhat verbosely entitled *Memoriale super visitatione domini Laurencii Ratholdi militis et baronis Vngarie, factum de Purgatorio sancti Patricii in insula Hibernie* ('A record concerning the visit of Lord Lawrence Rathold, knight and baron of Hungary, to the purgatory of St Patrick on the island of Ireland'). St Patrick's purgatory was a popular pilgrim destination from the twelfth to the sixteenth century (when the medieval site was destroyed), with numerous pilgrims travelling from all over Europe to visit the holy site. Rathold set out from Hungary on a lengthy pilgrimage to visit the great pilgrim destinations of Santiago de Compostela in Spain, and then St Patrick's purgatory in Ireland. He carried a letter of safe conduct from King

Sigismund of Hungary, who later became the king of Germany, Bohemia and Lombardy, as well as Holy Roman Emperor. The letter, written on 10 January 1408, described Rathold as the king's chief steward, 'a scion of the senior barons of our kingdoms, nurtured and known in our royal palace from his childhood and one found faithful and constant in numberless affairs, happy and unhappy'.[8] In 1413, soon after his return from Ireland, Rathold was sent to Venice as an emissary of King Sigismund.

Rathold's status as an eminent foreign nobleman made Yonge's commission highly significant. He arrived in Dublin with a herald and servants, and occupied his time in the city by visiting the major religious sites such as the cathedral of the Holy Trinity (Christ Church) and relics such as the Baculus Iesu – the crozier allegedly given by Christ to St Patrick with which he supposedly banished the snakes from Ireland. Rathold may have presented his letter of safe passage to members of the Dublin assembly and in this way have come into contact with Yonge. The Dubliner may have volunteered or been appointed to undertake the Hungarian's literary commission, and his fluent Latin and considerable literary abilities made him a suitable scribe for the task at hand. The text that Yonge produced was borne out of a series of conversations held with the Hungarian rather than direct dictation; Yonge claimed that he 'served the aforesaid knight in the capacity of secretary for many days and nights ... [and] many times discussed with the same knight by word of mouth individual events', while the Hungarian waited for a ship to take him to England where he was to meet with the English king Henry V on a diplomatic mission.[9] Yonge insisted that the work was written

> for the praise of God and also at the insistence of the aforesaid powerful men and for my spiritual benefit, [who] thought it suitable to faithfully compile and write this present history, as far as the grantor of all knowledge gave me ability, and according to the information given me by the aforementioned knight, leaving nothing out ...[10]

The text opens with a discussion of the history of the purgatory but also, perhaps owing to Yonge's awareness of the importance of documents, includes not only the letter of protection from Sigismund but also two certificates that certify Rathold's completion of the pilgrimage. The first document was a letter from the archbishop of Armagh, Nicholas Fleming, on 27 December 1411, which confirmed that Rathold, 'observing all and singular of the circumstances of that pilgrimage, devoutly entered the Purgatory of Saint Patrick ... truly penitent and armed with true faith'.[11] The second certificate was issued by Matthew, canon of the order of St Augustine and prior of the purgatory, on 12 November 1411 from Saint's Island in Lough Derg. This latter document details Rathold's actions, confirming his performance of penance, his attendance of mass, and describing how,

> having heard the mass of the Holy Cross and having observed other solemnities, and having fulfilled all of the requirements for the aforesaid pilgrimage as no other in our time has fulfilled them, naked and fasting, except for vestments and a breech-cloth, he bravely entered the cave of Saint Patrick with procession and litany[12]

Matthew recalled that he remained there fasting 'as long as practical' and recorded the pilgrim's vision of unclean spirits and divine revelations. These are our only evidence for such certificates of completion being produced and indeed provide much fascinating detail regarding the pilgrimage. Yonge's daily involvement in producing legal documentation for various reasons may have led him to include such official material into his account of the journey.

Yonge probably took some time to complete Rathold's account, but he did return to his day job where we can once again trace his involvement in various legal transactions. Several years later, in 1422, Yonge was again engaged for a literary commission, this time in English, for James Butler, fourth earl of Ormond. The text that he produced, the aforementioned *Gouernaunce of prynces*, is a translation of the *Secreta secretorum* ('The secret of secrets') that purported to be a handbook of advice given by Aristotle to the young Alexander the Great. (Only one full copy of Yonge's text survives along with one extract.) Translations of the *Secreta* were very popular throughout the Middle Ages – the aforementioned Thomas Hoccleve produced one such handbook for King Henry V in 1411–13. The text belonged to the genre of the 'mirrors for princes', providing the political elite with handbooks advising on the best ways to rule and keep hold of power. Such a text would have suited Ormond's tastes, since he cast himself in the mould of an effective military campaigner and the powerful chief governor of Ireland. After the obligatory dedication to God, the *Gouernaunce* text opens with an address to the patron:

> *... to yow, nobyll and gracious lorde, Iamys de Botillere, Erle of Ormonde, lieutenaunt of oure lege lorde, kynge henry the fyfte in Irland, humbly recommendyth hym youre pouer Seruant, Iames yonge, to youre hey lordshipp: altymes desyrynge in cryste, yowre honoure and profite of body and Sowle, and wyth al myn herte the trynyte afor-sayde beshechynge that he hit euer Encrese. Amen. Amen.*[13]

> ... to you, noble and gracious lord, James de Butler, earl of Ormond, lieutenant of our liege lord, king Henry the fifth in Ireland, humbly recommends [to] him your poor servant, James Yonge, to your high lordship: all times desiring in Christ, your honour and profit of body and soul, and with all my heart beseeching the aforesaid trinity that he it ever increase. Amen. Amen.

Butler – also known as the White Earl – was esteemed for his learning and patronage of literature in both English and Irish; the translation of the *Secreta* was probably commissioned to celebrate his first appointment to the position of lieutenant of Ireland in 1420–2. Again, it is important to note that when Yonge described himself as *youre pouer Seruant*, he was using the language of chivalry in order to appear humble and illustrate his respect and gratitude to the earl rather than to describe his actual position in relation to his patron and employer. This humble persona is part of the effort to flatter the earl, portraying Butler as a powerful, important and learned figure in Ireland. The book that he was translating and presenting imparted the sort of information that such a man should appreciate. In his defence of the translation, Yonge points out in the first chapter of the *Secreta* that the text demonstrates an important message for those who are in a position of power:

> *Chyuary is not only kepete, Sauyd and mayntenyd by dedys of armes, but by wysdome and helpe of lawes, and of witte, and wysdome of vndyrstondynge.*
> *But whan with Streynth and Powere, hym compaynyth witte and connynge, and witte dressith Powere, in goodnys may the Prynce Play, and with good men Surly walke.*[14]

Chivalry is not only kept, saved and maintained by deeds of arms, but by wisdom and help of laws, and of wit, and wisdom of understanding.

But when with strength and power, are combined with wit and cunning, and with guided power, in goodness may the prince play, and with good men surely walk.

He went on to say that

> *... Tully the grette clerke Sayth, 'than were wel gouernette Emperies and kyngdomes Whan kynges wer Phylosofors, and Philosofy regnyd.'*

... Tully the great man of letters [that is, the Roman statesman Marcus Tullius Cicero] says, 'there were well governed empires and kingdoms when kings were philosophers, and philosophy reigned'.

Well aware of the power of flattery, Yonge then exalts his patron, suggesting that it is Butler's own nobleness which drove him to desire such a manual:

The whyche thynge, nobil and gracious lorde afor-Sayde, haith Parcewid the Sotilte of youre witte, and the clernys of youre engyn, therfore I-chargid Some good boke of gouernaunce of Prynces out of latyn othyr Frenche in-to youre modyr Englyshe tonge to translate.

This thing, aforesaid noble and gracious lord, has been perceived by the skill of your wit, and the clearness of your engine [mind], therefore I was charged with translating some good book of governance of princes out of Latin or French into your mother English tongue.

Eager to highlight the illustrious genesis of the text recently translated for his patron, Yonge explained:

… now y here translate to youre Souerayne nobilnes the boke of arystotle, Prynce of Phylosofors, of the gouernaunce of Prynces, … The wych boke he makyd to his dysciple Alexandre the grete Emperoure, conqueroure of al the worlde.[15]

… now I here translate for your sovereign nobleness, the book of Aristotle, prince of philosophers, of 'the governance of princes', … The which book he [Aristotle] made for his disciple, Alexander the Great emperor, conqueror of all the world.

The original text on which Yonge's version was based was not in fact given to Alexander but was a medieval forgery drawn from an Arabic original. However, the text's status as a forgery was unknown in the late medieval world. The basic text was extremely popular in the Middle Ages and was translated into Latin, French and English and even rendered into Irish. Yonge's source was a thirteenth-century French text that had been translated from Latin by an Irish Dominican, Gofroi of Waterford, and Yonge freely adapted the prose to his purpose and his patron. The historian Elizabeth Matthew notes that Yonge's work involved 'blending his translation … with instances of Irish history', and he 'introduces current events pertaining to Irish history meant to flatter his patron'.[16] The manual purported to be an aid for Ormond in his governing of Ireland, and he may have enjoyed the opportunity offered by it to consult (or to appear to consult) the opinions of authoritative figures from antiquity in order to demonstrate his erudition as a late medieval nobleman. Along with its classical advice on how to rule effectively, the text also provided the earl with a summary of Irish history complete with an explanation of the authority by which the English king was entitled to rule Ireland.

Certain passages adapted in the translation display knowledge of Ormond's military campaigns and place them alongside the glories of Alexander the Great and the ancient heroes, allowing Yonge to write Ormond into the list of history's great men. Presenting Ormond and some of his ancestors as powerful military leaders, Yonge also acknowledges the role that God plays in war and thus underlines God's implicit support for Ormond's actions, since 'victory in battail Pryncipal is in god'. He explains that this is proved in

> *the deddis of the nobylle victorius Erle, Syr Iamys, yowre gravnde-Syre, whych in al his tyme lechury hatid: And ther-for god in al his tyme granted hym mervellous victori vp his enemys wyth fewe Pepill, Namly vp the morthes, of whyche he slew huge Pepill in the red more of athy, a litil afore the Sone goynge downe, stondynge the Sone mervelosly still till the slight was done.*[17]

> the deeds of the noble victorious earl, Sir James, your grandfather, which in all his time lechery hated: and therefore God in all his time granted him marvellous victories against his enemies with few people, namely on the Morthes [O'Mores?] of which he slew huge [numbers of] people in the red moor of Athy, a little before the sun went down, the sun standing marvellously still till the slaughter was done.[18]

This is probably the story of the victory of James Butler, the third earl and justiciar of Ireland, against the MacMurroughs and O'Mores of Laois in

1359.[19] For Yonge, and Ormond, victory on the battlefield was an important factor in maintaining control in Ireland. Yonge's text had little sympathy for Irish rebels and he advised Ormond to deal harshly with those who threatened the safety of the area loyal to the king:

> *Sethyn god and oure kynge haue grauntid you Powere, do ye therof Execucion in opyn fals enemys, traytouris, and rebelle, trew men quelleris, whan thay fallyth Into youre handys, by the thow Sharpe eggis of youre Swerde.*[20]

Since God and our king have granted you power, do therefore execute in [the] open: false enemies, traitors and rebels, killers of true men, when they fall into your hands, by the true sharp edge of your sword.

He goes on to highlight the importance of stamping out such rebels to prevent contagion:

> *For as a Sparke of fyre risyth an huge fyre able a realme to brente, So rysyth of the roote of an fals enemy, appert traytoure, othyr rebellis, many wickid wedis sone growynge, that al trewe men in londe Sore greuyth.*
> *... Therfor, whan thay fallyth into youre handis, Raase ham all out of rote, as the good gardyner dothe the nettylle.*[21]

For as a spark of fire raises a huge fire which can burn a realm, so rises out of the root of a false enemy, open traitors, other rebels, many wicked weeds soon grow, [so] that all true men in the land sadly grieve.
... Therefore, when they fall into your hands, tear them all out by the root, as the good gardener does [with] the nettle.

Yonge noted that certain English *captayns* of Ireland did not measure up to the required standard:

… god punyshid hame that chastenet not hare subiectis, me-thynketh hit apperyth oft-tymes by dyuers Englyshes captaynys o Irland that haue bene and now byth, whos neclygence in non-Punyshynge of hare nacionys and Subiectes haue destrued ham-Selfe, har naciones, and har landis.[22]

… God punished him that chastened not their subjects, I think it appears oftentimes by diverse English captains of Ireland that have been and are now [present], whose negligence in non-punishing their nations and subjects has destroyed themselves, their nation and their lands.

In this period, there was a long-running feud between two factions headed by the earl of Ormond (Yonge's patron) and Sir John Talbot, Lord Furnival, with both vying for control of the Irish government. Yonge was firmly in Ormond's camp: thus, when he noted that certain English *captayns* did not adequately punish wrongdoers, the implication is that Talbot was one such negligent captain while Ormond was the opposite. This comment would no doubt have pleased his patron and its inclusion may have been an attempt by Yonge to ingratiate himself with the earl in order to advance his own career.

The earl did not just make use of Yonge's literary skills, he also employed him for his administrative abilities. Yonge was among many of the earl's associates appointed to administrative positions during Ormond's 1420 lieutenantship, becoming second engrosser of the exchequer. The second engrosser of the exchequer was an assistant to the chief engrosser – basically a clerk or copyist responsible for keeping the official records of the exchequer on the great pipe roll, earning 5*d*. a day when the exchequer was open. Yonge did not complete this work himself, but in the custom of many appointees nominated a deputy, William Stokenbrick, to undertake the work on his behalf.[23]

Owing to his connections with Ormond, it was perhaps inevitable that Yonge would become embroiled in the factionalized politics of his time and in 1423, a few years after he had completed his *Gouernaunce* text for Ormond, Yonge was imprisoned by the pro-Talbot faction and sent to Trim Castle. This incarceration was almost certainly linked to the feud between Ormond and Talbot; it is unclear what crime he was charged with, but it was most likely connected to Talbot's decision to punish Ormond's supporters when he took power. Yonge was moved from Trim to Dublin Castle and eventually released to return to writing notarial instruments, but his connection to Ormond was not over. The earl employed him as a notary on a few occasions in the late 1420s and one of Ormond's first acts when he obtained the lieutenantship for the second time in 1425 was to grant Yonge a full pardon.

A few other traces of James Yonge can be found in the 1430s: on 5 November 1434 his long-standing client and friend John Lytill granted Yonge 20*s.* in his will for his work as executor. Given that this task was often completed by a family member, it may indicate a close friendship. In 1430 Yonge's hand appears in the founding charter of the guild of St Anne in St Audoen's parish; it became the largest religious guild in the city of Dublin with Yonge employed as one of its regular scribes. By this time, Yonge was nearing the end of his career as a professional scribe. Hereafter, references to James Yonge decline, and he appears to have been in semi-retirement by 1435, producing few documents and probably dying in 1439.

James Yonge's everyday legal work for the people of fifteenth-century Dublin stands alongside his literary creations for important visiting dignitaries and politicians. He dealt with the ordinary issues and arguments of medieval Dubliners, as well as being involved in a small way in the fierce factional struggles for power and control that engulfed the late medieval Irish political realm. As a writer and a professional, James Yonge's work offers an insight into the medieval world through this cross-section of experiences and realities from fifteenth-century Ireland. Through an examination of this fascinating character's life, work and circle, we are offered an opportunity to unlock stories drawn from everyday life in late medieval Dublin society and to augment our knowledge of the legal and literary history of the capital.

The Knight's Tale

SPARKY BOOKER

Christopher St Lawrence, the seventh baron of Howth, was born into an established English noble family of north Co. Dublin, probably sometime in the 1520s, just as the Middle Ages in Ireland were coming to a close. St Lawrence was part of a family that had been in Ireland, and indeed in the Dublin region, from the inception of the English colony in the late twelfth century. Almeric St Lawrence, the founder of the lineage, came to Ireland as a knight in the company of John de Courcy, his brother-in-law, in the late 1170s, and they had been landowners in Howth ever since that time, as de Courcy granted lands at Howth to Almeric as a reward for his service. The family controlled the harbour at Howth and took some portion of the merchandise and fish brought into that harbour, as well as having a right to the bodies of the whales and porpoises that washed ashore.[1] These suburban harbours, of which Co. Dublin had several, became increasingly lucrative as the Liffey silted up and became shallower in the later Middle Ages and was no longer as accessible to large ships that required deep anchorages. Dalkey, to the south, was probably the most important of these harbours, but Howth and the other harbours would also have increased in value as less traffic travelled down the Liffey. These harbours may have had lower rates of tax on incoming goods than Dublin, and attracted shipping in that way.[2] The harbour gave the St Lawrences a supplemental income to the rentals of their lands; it also gave them access to important visitors from England, who often came to Dublin through this harbour and may have stayed at Howth Castle, home of the St Lawrence family, on their arrival. For example, Richard, duke of York, arrived at Howth in 1449 to begin his tenure as the chief governor, the king's lieutenant and representative in

Ireland, as did Sir Edward Poynings, another fifteenth-century chief governor.[3] In the sixteenth century the earl of Sussex sailed into Howth, as did Sir Edward Bellingham and Sir James Croft: all of these men served as the king's representative in Ireland, the most powerful position in the administration of the lordship. The access to English officials that the harbour at Howth provided was probably helpful to St Lawrence family fortunes. These kinds of personal connection and direct access to very high-ranking officials would have been important in late medieval Ireland, where patronage determined so much in terms of political appointments and favour. Thus, the harbour and the lands around Howth provided a secure income and a sound political footing for the St Lawrence family throughout the Middle Ages (fig. 12.1).

Much of the information we have about this family comes from the Book of Howth, a work of history created by Christopher St Lawrence himself. The book was compiled in the 1570s and was probably dictated by St Lawrence to several hired scribes. The use of scribes was common and St Lawrence's nickname, 'the blind lord', suggests that he had poor eyesight and

12.1 Howth Castle, from W.H. Bartlett, N.P. Willis and J. Stirling Coyne, *The scenery and antiquities of Ireland*, vol. ii (London, 1842).

might not have wished to write the entire work himself. His hand does appear in some marginalia, however, so he did occasionally write on the manuscript himself, though only brief notes.[4] The survival of this book is one reason that we know so much about the St Lawrences compared to other similar families. Christopher used the book to glorify his ancestors and he exaggerated their role in the conquest of Ireland and wrote many passages that depicted them as noble, strong and brave. He described Almeric, his progenitor and founder of the St Lawrences in Ireland, in this way:

> amongst a thousand knights Sir Amory [Almeric] might be chosen for beauty, stout-stomachness and stalworthness; for he was stout and sturdy to his peer, and humble and full of courtesy to his inferiors.[5]

Of John de Courcy, Almeric's brother-in-law, he wrote:

> one who had seen Sir John that day, being not in fear or danger, might say he was alter ercules [another Hercules]. He fought that day with a two-handed sword more like a lion than a lamb; his blows were so weighty and so to be wondered at that it was very strange to behold, for there was never a blow he strack but slew a man.[6]

St Lawrence clearly took some poetic licence and, accordingly, we should not trust the particulars about these earlier lords of Howth. Nevertheless, his family was an important one in the English colony in Ireland and, like so many established settler families, their military and administrative service helped not just to win, but to ensure the survival of the colony in the face of the myriad challenges of the later Middle Ages. The St Lawrences were also a remarkably fertile family. From the start of their lineage with Almeric until the time of Christopher and beyond, they continued in a direct male line without land going to heiresses or being split up between different heirs, and this unbroken succession was vital to the stability of the family. In addition to serving in the administration of the colony, the St Lawrences were frequently involved in the defence of the English colony from attacks by the Irish, and thus they were more militarily active than comparable noble families in England. This was the case despite the fact that their ancestral lands and home were located in the heart of the region that by the late fifteenth century was called the Pale. This refers to a crescent of land running from around Dundalk in the north to Dalkey in the south; it was the area most firmly under the control of the Dublin administration in this period.

An earlier Christopher St Lawrence, the fourteenth lord and first baron of Howth, advanced the family's fortunes in the mid-fifteenth century. He received a knighthood from the crown and served as a member of the king's council in Ireland in the 1450s. Christopher's son Robert was also active in the colonial administration and was appointed chancellor of Ireland in 1483. He served in this post for only a short time, however, since he encountered resistance to his appointment from the king's deputy-lieutenant in Ireland, the powerful eighth earl of Kildare, who wished to keep the position for his brother.[7] Robert's son Nicholas – our knight's grandfather – was also chancellor for a short time. The family continued to rise in prominence, as they proved politically adept enough to navigate the complex factional politics of fifteenth-century Ireland. Yet another Christopher, the fourth baron of Howth and father of our subject, continued the family tradition of administrative and military service in the colony and served as sheriff of Dublin.[8] He had three sons – Edward, Richard and Christopher. Christopher was the youngest of the three, but the death of both of his older brothers without heirs meant that he became the lord and baron of Howth – titles that, as a third son, he probably did not imagine he would ever hold.

Christopher was born sometime in the 1520s: although we know a great deal about him, his actual birth date is not recorded. He grew up at Howth Castle, a member of the tight-knit settler community of the Pale. He was a Palesman on both sides, since his mother was a Bermingham, also from a very long-established settler family based in Co. Kildare. The tomb of Christopher's great-great grandfather, who died in 1462, shows the connections and links that his family had with other Pale families. This tomb is in St Mary's Church, the ruins of which sit on the hill at Howth, overlooking the harbour (figs 12.2, 12.3). The tomb depicts the lord of Howth and his wife and is decorated with their coats of arms and those of their relations, including the prominent Pale families of Plunkett, Cusack and Fleming. The St Lawrences were linked by marriage to these families and they were keen to display these connections on the personal and long-lasting monument of their tomb. In contrast to many other settler families, even within the Pale, there is no evidence that they married Irish people and they seemed intent on marrying within the English community.

We know little of Christopher St Lawrence's childhood or early life, but he went to England as a young man and we know that he was being

12.2 Christopher St Lawrence's tomb 1, St Mary's Collegiate Church, Howth: tomb-surround (© Edwin Rae collection, TRIARC, Irish Art Research Centre).

12.3 Christopher St Lawrence's tomb 2, St Mary's Collegiate Church, Howth: tomb-surround, detail (© Edwin Rae collection, TRIARC, Irish Art Research Centre).

educated at Lincoln's Inn in London in 1554. Lincoln's Inn was one of several inns of court that trained lawyers in English law, and going there was a common educational path for the sons of prominent families of the English of Ireland, particularly since the colony did not have its own university until the founding of Trinity College in 1592. This legal education at the inns prepared these sons of English Ireland for positions in the administration of the colony and, just as importantly, reinforced their cultural and political links with England. St Lawrence's time in England did not all run smoothly and in 1554 he was threatened with expulsion from the Inn for wearing a beard.[9] The inns imposed certain standards of dress and behaviour on their members and infractions like this, as well as more serious crimes, were not unusual.[10] St Lawrence, however, may have encountered more serious conflicts with his English classmates and colleagues. There is evidence that many of the English in England did not trust the English of Ireland and did not consider them to be true Englishmen. Animosity and distrust between these two English communities grew in the late Middle Ages. Englishmen mocked the provincial accents and clothes of the colonists, and accused them of intermingling with the native Irish and departing from English norms and civilized behaviour. This was reflected at the inns of court. In Lincoln's inn, where St Lawrence studied, there were occasional bans on 'Irish' fellows and there was at one point a limit on how many 'Irish' people could live in one house there at the same time.[11] The very terminology of these bans would have been offensive to men such as St Lawrence, who would have considered the term 'Irish' as a slander. It was such a serious insult within the English colony that settlers took one another to court and sued for damages if they were wrongfully accused of being Irish.

This difference in terminology reveals a great deal about the divergent perspectives of these two English communities: the English of Ireland generally described themselves as English, while the English in England often used the word 'Irish' indiscriminately to describe all of the inhabitants of Ireland, settler and native alike. This discrimination was also apparent in the larger arena of national politics, since the Irish, meaning in this context all people from Ireland, were included in aliens' taxes in 1440. These were taxes that non-Englishmen living in England had to pay. Nevertheless, the English of Ireland objected so strenuously to the tax, and to the implication that they were not English, that it was revoked a few years later.[12] This anti-Irish feeling in England seems to have made its mark on St Lawrence, and may have influenced his later political decisions and the views that he expressed in the Book of Howth.

When St Lawrence returned to Ireland from London in the 1550s he became involved in the Dublin administration in various roles, acting as an advisor and administrator. On the death of his brother Richard in 1558 he took the family title of lord of Howth and in 1561 he was granted the title of baron of Howth. He became a favourite of Sussex, the chief governor of Ireland from 1556 to 1564, and was loyal to him, helping with his campaigns in Ulster against Shane O'Neill. St Lawrence travelled back to England in

1562 with several other Palesmen to present letters to Queen Elizabeth detailing what was going on in Ireland and advising her on Irish affairs.[13] Presumably this indicates that he had become reasonably well respected in the settler community by this time, for he was entrusted with such a delicate task. This trip went well, and the men talked and debated with the queen at length. Yet when he related the story of this visit in the Book of Howth, St Lawrence wrote that the queen asked him whether he could speak the English tongue, which would have been a deeply insulting question for a man from a community that vehemently asserted its Englishness.[14] It is difficult to credit that Elizabeth did not know that this English-educated nobleman could speak English, but it is probable that she was teasing him, while at the same time putting him firmly in his place. In any case, he must have dealt with the insult well enough, since he remained in favour and received a knighthood several years later in 1570.

St Lawrence continued his work in the Dublin administration, although he began increasingly to come into conflict with the crown and the crown's representatives in Ireland. There were a few issues at hand. Firstly there was growing mutual distrust and at times even animosity between the English of Ireland and the English of England. This was reflected in the fact that in the second half of the sixteenth century the crown increasingly sent English officials to fill posts in Ireland, rather than relying on the colonial community in Ireland to serve in these positions, which had been the norm in the Middle Ages. Predictably, this caused friction, as such attempts at centralization had done throughout the medieval period. Palesmen – men such as St Lawrence and his friends and relations – felt that it was their right to govern Ireland and reacted angrily when their control was threatened. They appealed to their history to justify their privileged position in Ireland and they translated Gerald of Wales, the twelfth-century commentator on the invasion of Ireland, to show that their ancestors had won the colony with their blood and their sweat, and that they, the descendants of these conquerors, deserved to control it. The Book of Howth is a good example of these attempts to justify and validate the position of the settler community, although there are many others. In the book, St Lawrence emphasized the valour that his family and their allies displayed in winning the colony and defending it throughout the Middle Ages. This was not mere self-indulgence, but rather proof that without the Old English, as the settlers came to be called, the colony would not exist. In contrast to the brave, noble and deserving Palesmen in the Book of Howth, newer arrivals from England – the so-called New English – were depicted as dishonest and grasping. A contemporary of St Lawrence wrote about these officials – new arrivals to Ireland – saying that they were greedy and

> sought nothing else but a spoil and continuance of service, advancing themselves in the court of England with painted garments and massy chains of the ill-gotten gains of Ireland ... adding to their shameless craving, slanderous lies of poor Ireland.[15]

The Book of Howth features several of these English officials. One was a Mr Coule, whom the book claims, significantly, was 'born in England'. The account of Coule (Robert Crowley, d. *c.*1546) claims that, although he served on the council of the eighth earl of Kildare, he was dismissed from the ninth earl's council in *c.*1513–15. Angry at his dismissal, he became the ninth earl's enemy and 'wrought as much against the earl of Kildare as he could or was able'. According to St Lawrence, he succeeded in his revenge, fomenting Silken Thomas' rebellion by complaining about the ninth earl of Kildare to King Henry VIII's Privy Council in the 1530s.[16] The Book of Howth sets the scene, as

> this Coule was in England before the Council, complaining about the earl, and tears fell from his eyes. The earl asked him why he was crying. He said it was for pity that he had for the earl, whose father he had served, but that his duty to the king forced him to treat Kildare in this way. The earl said in response 'he is like the plover taker who sets his snares, and waits for his desired purpose ... All the plovers as he takes, he knocks their brains out with his thumb, notwithstanding his watery tears of contemplation. Mr Coule does

the same with me; his tears cometh down, but he lays shrewd matters or articles against me'.[17]

Coule, as depicted here, was the perfect example of the New Englishman in the Old English imagination: he is scheming, hypocritical and disingenuous, a foil to the loyal, truthful Old English earl of Kildare. The earl's clever analogy of the plover catcher got him out of trouble with the king, but when he was incapacitated with an injury, Coule took advantage and proceeded with his 'evil disposed purpose', as the Book of Howth puts it. He attacked the earl's character and ensured that he was imprisoned in the Tower of London, putting the events into motion that led to the revolt of Silken Thomas, the earl's son, in 1534. In this instance, as in many others, we can see St Lawrence manipulating history to blame the New English for the revolt of the Old English. He did not want to admit that any of the Old English community, led by Silken Thomas, would have rebelled against the crown unless they were duped and misrepresented by this New English snake in the grass.

There was also an element of snobbery in the Old English objections to people like Coule; often these administrators were not of noble blood, making their replacement of members from very old Norman noble families even more insulting. Old English authors denigrated the common birth of these officials and accused them of money-grubbing and self-interest. The New English, on the other hand, accused the Old English of being degenerate and disloyal. Edmund Spenser's famous (and often misquoted) accusation that the settlers had 'degenerated and growen almost meare Irishe; yea, and more malicious to the Englishe than the very Irishe themselves' is an example of such claims.[18] St Lawrence reacted angrily to these accusations of disloyalty. He included a long list of English traitors, literally hundreds and hundreds of names taken from throughout English history, in the Book of Howth. He justified the list by saying that it was

A number of the nobility, gentlemen, and commons of England that hath rebelled against their natural prince since William

Conqueror's time; also thousands more I do overpass, for the tediousness of time, which I do omit. The occasion of this remembrance is, for that when any of the English birth come to Ireland, they report and brag that all therein … are traitors, as who would say and affirm that there was never any treason committed in England. The truth is that no country that is known ever rebelled more against their prince than England; so hereby you understand the cause of this rehearsal.[19]

There was another, more specific, issue that strained St Lawrence's relationship with the English administration – cess. Cess is the name of a specific kind of tax used in later medieval and early modern Ireland. The so-called cess controversy that raged in Ireland in the 1560s and 1570s arose from the use of this tax by many chief governors who used it to pay for their armies. It had originally been a once-off tax for exceptional circumstances rather than a continual imposition, but it was used frequently and was very onerous in this period. It allowed chief governors to take goods and money from the English of Ireland without any legislative justification (that is, without the approval of the Irish parliament) since it was considered an extension of royal prerogative. St Lawrence asserted the illegality of continual and unlegislated cess, which he called a 'great and unreasonable charge' and moreover one without ancient precedent. He always maintained that, despite his opposition to the cess, he was a loyal subject of the queen. He complained frequently against cesses in the Book of Howth and used them as a yardstick to rate various deputies, arguing that one was a good governor because he did not often exact cess, while another was a bad governor because he did. He recounted the journey of several Palesmen to the queen to object to cess, whereupon they were imprisoned 'for that they spake against the Queen's prerogative, as it was supposed. But truly', he argued,

they neither spake ne thought anything against the prerogative, but declared the charges that were levied upon the country by reason of the cesse … which continued these 28 years past; by reason thereof the realm was utterly decayed and impoverished.[20]

The queen would not yield in this matter and insisted that it was her prerogative to levy this tax whenever she liked. St Lawrence and several of his fellow objectors were eventually imprisoned for their opposition to cess in May 1577 and were held in Dublin Castle, where they were questioned and told that they must give in. They refused and maintained that they were loyal subjects and had no interest in denying the queen's rights, but that their community could not handle the burden of cess. They were released in 1578 after many months of imprisonment and had not reneged on their opposition. In the following year, 1579, St Lawrence's tumultuous personal life intruded and these political activities were put on hold.

St Lawrence had continued the family policy of marrying into other Old English Pale families when he married Elizabeth Plunkett, of the Plunkett family of Louth, in 1546. The couple had fourteen children, but only six of these survived to adulthood and he seems to have had a hand in one of their premature deaths. Despite this multitude of children, his marriage to Plunkett was not a happy one and the conflict in his immediate family came to a head in 1579. In this year he was prosecuted in the court of the castle chamber for violent assaults on his own family. Witnesses testified that he led a very immoral life, had 'filthy conversation' and visited what were euphemistically called 'strange women'. The court charged that

> it also appeared that by this his usual haunting and keeping of hores, his wife became so hateful to him as he could not without striking and beating of her sufficiently satisfy the cruelty of his mind.[21]

This background about his sexual proclivities was just unsavoury detail to strengthen the case against St Lawrence; the real issue in court was the violence he had perpetrated against his own family. He had allegedly beaten his wife very badly on two occasions and on one of these, the court noted, he stripped her naked to beat her. He also tied his butler to a post and beat him, after the servant had tried to give his wife something to eat. When his thirteen-year-old daughter went to Dublin without his permission, he assaulted her so severely that she died soon after the incident.[22] At this time, hitting one's wife, children or servants would not have been illegal, or even particularly frowned upon. It was considered a legitimate way for the head of a household to correct the faults of his supposed inferiors. There is apparently not much proof for the common assertion that our phrase 'rule of thumb' comes from an English medieval custom whereby men could strike their wives with a stick that was no thicker than his thumb; however, this does correspond well to the medieval attitude to hitting one's wife. It was entirely acceptable as long as the punishment was reasonable and measured and did not cause a serious or mortal injury. St Lawrence's alleged behaviour was very clearly outside this norm, both in the severity of the wounds suffered by his wife and daughter and also in the very irrationality and cruelty of his actions. This was not the reasonable correction that medieval jurists felt was appropriate. Rather, it was an out of control, enraged frenzy.

Accordingly, the court punished St Lawrence heavily with an enormous fine of £1,000. Just to put this fine in context, in the five years before 1579 the annual revenue of the Irish exchequer averaged only £4,305.[23] The jury noted that St Lawrence deserved death for what he had done, but his aristocratic connections made such a punishment unlikely, particularly since he had assaulted only members of his own family. Later, either as the scandal died down or as it became clear that he could never pay such a sum, the fine was halved to £500, which he probably did not pay off either. One reason for this huge fine, apart from the terrible nature of his crime, may have been to ensure that he was in debt to the government, and this would have been a way to control him and prevent him from doing things such as organizing resistance to government actions, as he had done when resisting the cess. In fact, Valerie McGowan-Doyle, who has written extensively on St Lawrence, has argued that the court case was undertaken to silence and discredit St Lawrence, so that his opposition to cess would end. This reading of the court case is convincing, since, although St Lawrence probably did beat his wife, daughter and servant, the huge, unpayable fine that he was given for the offence does support the idea that this court case was used opportunistically by the English administration in Ireland to silence him.

As one might imagine, Elizabeth Plunkett left St Lawrence in 1579 and he remarried, choosing Cecily Cusack, daughter of another Old English family of the Pale. He reconciled with the Dublin administration and began again to be appointed to positions within it – even a seat in the court of castle chamber, the very court that had tried him. He did not participate in any of the rebellions of the 1580s and stayed loyal to the queen. He did not display any signs of opposing the Protestant reformation that was being enforced more and more in Ireland, and the Book of Howth is almost completely silent on religious matters. There is evidence that his family may have continued to practise Catholicism privately, but St Lawrence did not publicly challenge the state religion. Thus, despite their earlier disagreements, St Lawrence was on good terms with the government, a loyal subject and Englishman, at his death in 1589.

So what should we think of St Lawrence? He seems to have been a violent man, as well as quarrelsome, self-aggrandizing and intensely proud, and in many important ways he was, apparently, a despicable character. Nevertheless, the vulnerability that he shows in the Book of Howth, his deep-seated defensiveness and fear in the face of the frightening changes of the sixteenth century that threatened the very existence of his community as he knew it, make it difficult not to sympathize with him. He was one of the last of the medieval Palesmen, born just as the Middle Ages in Ireland were ending, and one can sense his desperation as he tried to maintain the position that he and his friends and family had held for centuries in Ireland, clinging to his relationship with the crown and to his own stridently English identity, which was being constantly called into question. His life spans a fascinating period in Irish history, as the privileged position of the Old English crumbled away and their community was faced with alienation from the crown, loss of status and position, and a frightening and uncertain future.

1 (above) View of South Great George's Street site looking north: note Dubhlinn gardens in rear (photograph by Kevin Weldon).

2 The shield boss excavated at South Great George's Street (photograph by John Sunderland).

3 Reaping corn from the Luttrell Psalter, England, *c.*1320–40
(© The British Library Board, BL, Add. MS 42130, fo. 172v).

4 Gathering corn from the Luttrell Psalter, England, *c.*1320–40
(© The British Library Board, BL, Add. MS 42130, fo. 173r).

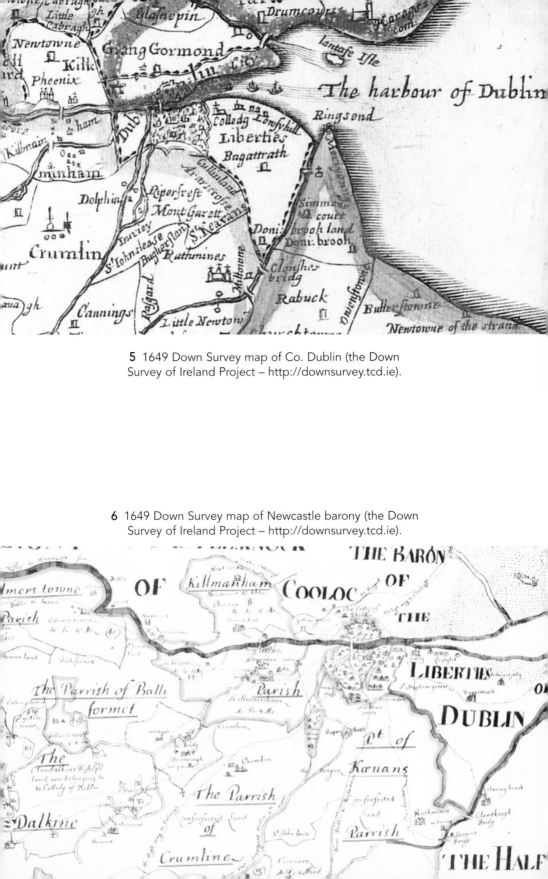

5 1649 Down Survey map of Co. Dublin (the Down Survey of Ireland Project – http://downsurvey.tcd.ie).

6 1649 Down Survey map of Newcastle barony (the Down Survey of Ireland Project – http://downsurvey.tcd.ie).

7 Detail of a miniature of a city officer with a key, a measure and a purse
(© The British Library Board, BL, Royal 19 C XI, fo. 39v).

8 Women tending sheep from the Luttrell Psalter, England, *c.*1320–40
(© The British Library Board, BL, Add. MS 42130, fo. 163v).

9 A fifteenth-century depiction of the Irish exchequer from the 'Red Book of the Irish Exchequer' in J.T. Gilbert (ed.), *Facsimiles of national manuscripts of Ireland, selected and edited under the direction of the Right Hon. Edward Sullivan, master of the rolls in Ireland* (4 pts in 5 vols, Dublin, 1874–84), iii, pl. 37.

10 The Wife of Bath from Chaucer's *Canterbury Tales* from Huntington Library MS Ellesmere 26 C 9, fo. 72r (© Huntington Library).

11 Scale model of Dublin, *c.*1500, viewed from the south, with
a) Dublin Castle in the south-east corner of the walled town,
b) St Patrick's Cathedral outside the southern limits of the walled area,
and c) the bridge over the Liffey to the north-west (© Dublinia).

12 James Malton's 'View of the law-courts', looking up the Liffey, Dublin (© National Library of Ireland).

13 Seal of the provostship of Dublin, RIA, MS 12.S.22–31, no. 599, 1459 (by permission of the Royal Irish Academy © RIA).

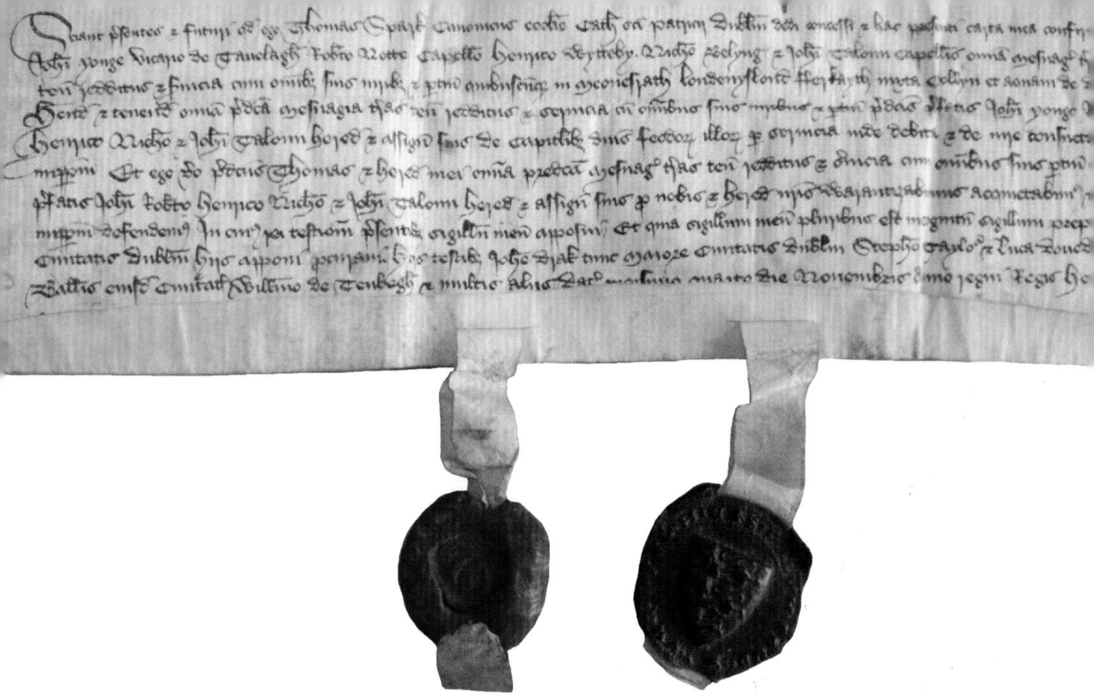

14 James Yonge's earliest extant document, National Library MS D7772 (© National Library of Ireland).

15 (*above left*) Detail of a miniature of a scribe with a quill, a knife, shears, a pen-case and an inkpot (© The British Library Board, BL, Royal 19 C XI, fo. 27v).
16 (*above right*) The Man of Law from Chaucer's *Canterbury Tales*, Huntington Library, MS Ellesmere 26C9, fo. 50v (© Huntington Library).

The Man of Law's Tale

COLM LENNON

To most people, James Stanihurst's (1522–73) claim to fame is that he was the father of Richard, the notable author, who composed histories of Ireland in English and Latin, wrote several works of Counter-Reformation devotion, and translated Virgil's *Aeneid* into English hexameters. More than half of Richard's life was spent away from his native country, as a Catholic exile in the Spanish Netherlands. He also had a sojourn at the Escorial palace in Spain where he was physician to King Philip II. Richard later became a priest and was chaplain at the court in Brussels, where he died in 1618 at the age of 71. By contrast, his father, James Stanihurst's biography was more pedestrian, at least on the face of it. He lived most of his life in or near Dublin, where he died prematurely at the age of 51, and pursued his avocation as lawyer more or less exclusively. Yet, his tale provides an important insight into the period of rapid political and religious change of the mid-Tudor years. In examining the details of his legal career, we see the loyal servant of city and state presented with sharp conflicts of loyalties. We also find a committed humanist and reformer who believed in a peaceful and educational approach to the challenge of bringing moral and social change to the communities of Ireland. Moreover, he put his knowledge of Irish history and law at the disposal of his son and his guest, Edmund Campion, as they researched and wrote a very influential work on the country's past.

The family into which James Stanihurst was born about 1522 had been prominent in municipal life in Dublin for several generations. The Stanihursts also had a strong sense of English civility and culture that had shaped the community of the Pale in eastern Ireland. In both spheres –

those of municipal and colonial government – the Stanihursts proved their commitment by their loyal service as administrators and officials, and James was to carry on these traditions. His grandfather, another Richard, who was mayor of Dublin in 1489, died as a wealthy man in 1501 and James' father, Nicholas, held the mayoralty in 1543. Nicholas also served the state in the 1530s and 1540s as a clerk in the court of chancery in Dublin Castle. As their standing in civic and colonial society was raised, the Stanihursts married into some of the substantial gentry and mercantile families of the English Pale, such as the Marewards and the Passavaunts. Besides their public service, the Stanihursts demonstrated their engagement with the Old English milieu in Ireland by nourishing its roots through educational migration. Mayor Richard Stanihurst's two sons were students in England at the time of his death in 1501 and one of them, John, was referred to as a scholar of Oxford. Through their education at university and law-school in London, the Stanihursts, and their fellow Palesmen, were opened to the new political and religious movements of Renaissance England.

At the time of James' birth, the Stanihursts' city home was probably in the tower embedded in the south-western wall of Dublin that came to bear their name as Stanihurst's tower (fig. 13.1). Nicholas, his father, was credited with repairing the bridge at the nearby Pole Gate, which spanned the Poddle river. The first mention we have of James as a youth is in the chronicle of the revolt of Silken Thomas Fitzgerald in 1534, when he is mentioned as one of a group of children from Dublin families who had been evacuated to the countryside for safety but were seized as hostages by the rebels. For the youngster, this brush with the revolt was a foretaste of the far-reaching changes that would follow the demise of the Kildare Fitzgeralds as the dominant force in Irish politics. At some stage in the late 1530s or early 1540s, James was sent by his parents to study in England, where he attended law-school in London, possibly at Gray's inns. In later years, Sir William Cecil, chief secretary of Queen Elizabeth (and Stanihurst's exact contemporary), remembered having met him there and having formed a favourable opinion of him. Some time in his early twenties, James married Anne Fitzsimon, daughter of Thomas of Swords, who was recorder or city

13.1 Stanihurst's tower at far left, from Richard Stanihurst's 'The historie of Irelande' in Holinshed's *Chronicles*, 1577 edition (© Huntington Library).

attorney for Dublin, and, with her, he had three sons, including Richard who was born in 1547. They also had a daughter, Margaret, who married Arland Ussher, a merchant of the city, and who was the mother of the famous scholar, James Ussher, who became the Church of Ireland archbishop of Dublin.

It was very much through his family connections that opportunities came to James to embark on his career of public service to the city and the state. His first appointment in 1547 – as receiver and collector of customs in the ports of Dublin and Drogheda – was specifically as 'the son of Nicholas Stanihurst'. When his father-in-law, Thomas Fitzsimon, became too ill to carry out the duties of recorder of Dublin, James was appointed *pro tempore* and then as permanent holder of the office in 1554. The recorder was the principal legal officer of the civic community who held the office for life at an annual salary of £30. In this role, James was expected to preside as judge at the city court and to offer counsel to the mayor and corporation whenever they consulted him. His state service began as joint-holder with his father of the office of clerk of the crown in chancery, another lifetime appointment and suitable for one qualified in the law. He also became clerk of the parliament in succession to his father in 1556. Recognition of his legal

and constitutional knowledge and fair dealing came by way of his appointment by the government as speaker of the House of Commons in three
parliaments, that of Queen Mary in 1557 and those of Queen Elizabeth in
1560 and 1569–71. It was in this position that he was called upon to make a
decisive contribution to the smooth implementation of political and
religious reforms under the Tudor monarchy.

As a reward for their loyalty in the early years of the Reformation under
Henry VIII, members of the Pale community had received grants of former
monastic property. Nicholas Stanihurst had been awarded the site and
possessions of the White Friars monastery to the south of the walls of
Dublin, close to the family base near the Pole Gate (no. 39 on Speed's map
above, p. ii). In the county of Meath, the former nunnery of Odder with
its 110-acre estate was conveyed to Nicholas on a twenty-one-year lease.
From the municipality of Dublin, which had been granted by Henry VIII
the monastic possessions of All Hallows or All Saints to the east of the walls,
came the farm of the revenues of the extensive estates throughout Dublin
county. James inherited most of these gains in the city and countryside,
consolidating the family fortunes and receiving further properties himself.
A grateful city council awarded their recorder a lease of the Pole mill, a
water mill on the Poddle river in Little Ship Street, and also the villages of
Donnycarney and Ballycullen in Co. Dublin. Coinciding with his rise to
prominence, James seems to have acquired the status of gentleman, as he
established a county seat and estate at Corduff, 10km to the north of
Swords in Co. Dublin. This allowed him to maintain his links with the
municipality, while at the same time cultivating relations with the gentry of
the surrounding north county region, including the Fitzsimons of Swords
and the Barnewalls of Turvey.

The appointment of James as speaker to preside over the periodic
meetings of the Irish parliament was carefully thought out by the governing
authorities. In 1557, at the assembly held under Queen Mary, one of the
principal items on the agenda was the restoration of the Roman Catholic
religion as the official one within the state. After a turn towards
Protestantism under Mary's half-brother, Edward VI, who died in 1553, a

complete change of direction back towards Rome was being planned. Not only were the rites and practices of the older religion restored, but the supremacy of the pope over ecclesiastical matters was also re-established. This link had been broken for Ireland in 1536 under Henry VIII, though he had not actually embraced the doctrines of the Protestant reformers. One of the decisive actions undertaken by Henry, however, was the dissolution of the monasteries. In acknowledgment of the support of the local political community of the Pale and the towns, including the Stanihursts, the lands and properties of the monks, friars and nuns had been redistributed to them, as we have seen. Now, in 1557, parliament was ready to acquiesce in the restoration of the Catholic religion, but no proposal was made to re-endow the religious orders, though St Patrick's Church, Dublin, was restored to its cathedral status. Thus, James Stanihurst oversaw a relatively uncontroversial religious measure, which ended, for the moment, the brief dalliance with state Protestantism.

The next parliament in 1560, called by Queen Elizabeth, was to represent another complete reversal of religious policy and the question of the speakership was again carefully considered. The government weighed the merits of both James Stanihurst and Thomas Cusack, the lord chancellor, as suitable candidates, but settled on the choice of Stanihurst. The only items of legislation were the measures to establish Protestantism as the religion of the state, to which all the subjects of the queen (who was to be supreme governor of the Church of Ireland) were obliged to conform. Unlike the proceedings of 1557, where the restoration of Catholicism was apparently not contentious, some parliamentarians were opposed to the new regime in religion. The parliamentary session lasted only three weeks, by which time the proposals had become law. In the aftermath, it was claimed that James Stanihurst, as the loyal agent of the government, had used subterfuge to have the laws passed. One version was that he convened parliament on St Brigid's day, a traditional holiday in Ireland when most of the members were away, and that he got a promise from the authorities that the measures would not be enforced. There may have been an element of later propaganda by Catholic apologists who, faced with the unpleasant reality that their parents' generation may have acquiesced in the Elizabethan Reformation, chose Speaker Stanihurst as a scapegoat. Thus, he was branded 'sly' and 'ambitious'. Whatever the truth of it, there is no doubt that James acted the part of the loyal servant of the state and oversaw the reversal of the previously passed religious legislation that he himself had mediated.

What do we know about James Stanihurst's personal religious convictions? In keeping with his willingness to be the medium for change from Catholicism to Protestantism, James subscribed to the oath of supremacy as was required of a state official. In the early years of the reign of Queen Elizabeth, adherence to the reformed religion was perhaps a political rather than a confessional statement and members of the Old English community have been characterized as 'church papists'. That means that they conformed publicly to the rites of the Anglican state church, but in private adhered to the practices of the old Catholic faith. Among the contemporaries of James Stanihurst were fellow legists and officials such as Chancellor Thomas Cusack and Chief Justice John Plunket, whose religious positions were ambivalent. Not until the 1570s and afterwards were believers compelled to commit definitively to one confession or the other, given the deep ideological divisions opened up by religious wars and conflict. There are two testimonies to James' secret commitment to Catholicism despite his public face. One is that of his son, Richard, admittedly a biased commentator, who in the late 1570s averred that James had been 'very Catholic', as he put it, and had turned down the chancellorship of Ireland because of his reluctance to commit himself fully to the Reformation. Meanwhile, in the last year of James' life, as he petitioned the English court for further preferment, the Protestant archbishop of Dublin, Adam Loftus, feared that James Stanihurst, while notable for his honesty, was 'not soundly or faithfully persuaded in religion', which was code for Catholic in outlook.[1]

Perhaps a better way of looking at James' mentality is to study his intellectual and cultural attitudes, which grew out of his legal career. There is no doubt that he was seen as having integrity and soundness of judgment but, more than that, he was genuinely interested in learning and scholarship as a means of advancing his community and that of the Gaelic Irish. On the occasion of the third of the parliaments over which he presided in 1569–71, he held forth on the benefits of a law that had just been passed for the setting up of an endowed grammar school in each diocese of Ireland. James regarded the measure as vital for the spreading of the 'pure English tongue, habit, fashion and discipline' throughout the country, and the weaning away of the Irish from uncivil practices. He continued:

> Surely might one generation sip a little of this liquor [of education], and so be induced to long for more, that both our countrymen that live obeisant would ensue with a corage the fruits of peace, whereby good learning is supported, and our unquiet neighbours would find such sweetness in the taste thereof as it should be a ready way to reclaim them.[2]

James Stanihurst was here reflecting a belief in reform through education that stemmed from the Christian humanist movement of Erasmus and Thomas More. In the course of his oration to parliament, Stanihurst lamented the failure of a scheme to establish a university in Ireland, which had many well-wishers, including the chief governor, Sir Henry Sidney, who had contributed money and gave his backing to the proposed college. Such an academic foundation was delayed for a further twenty years, until the opening of Trinity College.

James Stanihurst's words as speaker of parliament in 1571 were recorded by his house-guest of some months, the noted English scholar, Edmund Campion. The Englishman had come to Dublin to escape the pressure of conformity to the Anglican church and stayed in the city home of James and his son, Richard, who had been befriended by Campion as a student at Oxford. During his seven-month sojourn in Dublin and later in Turvey, Co. Dublin, Campion researched and wrote a history of Ireland with the help of Speaker Stanihurst and his son, Richard. In a preface to the work, he mentioned the 'daily table talk' of James as having been particularly helpful to his endeavour, and he paid tribute to the cultivated atmosphere of the Stanihurst household in a letter of thanks to James:

You sated me with every pleasure of place, season and company. You set me up with a library of books drawn from your own and you provided so admirably that I should have ease and opportunity for study, that may I perish if I ever conversed so sweetly with the muses outside of Oxford's walls.[3]

Among the sources to which Campion had access in Stanihurst's library were official documents, statute rolls and chronicles, as well as manuscripts and books, including a version of Giraldus Cambrensis' works. There is no doubt that his Irish stay provided Campion with a pleasant respite from the pressures in England, but it has been speculated that the purpose of his visit was to take a leading role in the proposed university college at Dublin that was being supported by Sidney, Stanihurst and other leading members of the Dublin community. Such an academic foundation at that time would not only have cultivated native learning but would also perhaps have avoided the confessional rigidity associated with Trinity College in its early years.

Richard Stanihurst's precocious scholarly talent, as seen during his undergraduate career at Oxford and which drew Campion to Dublin, was nourished by his grammar school master, Peter White. On a number of occasions in his writing, Richard Stanihurst attributed his own scholarly and literary success to the influence of White, who ran a grammar school in the grounds of St Canice's Cathedral in Kilkenny. James Stanihurst chose the Kilkenny academy for his son's education on the basis of the excellence of the pedagogy of White and the innovativeness of the master's methodology and curriculum. The speaker would no doubt have had White in mind as the model exemplar of the programme for reform in education that he propounded in his manifesto in parliament in 1571. Richard characterized the training there as a mixing of 'study with recreation, sorrow with mirth, paine with pleasure, sowerness with sweetness, roughness with mildness' in 'framing the education to the scholar's vaine'.[4] From this grammar school in Kilkenny and its successor that White ran at Waterford, there emerged ('as if from a Trojan horse', according to Richard) some of the leading lights of the Irish Counter-Reformation, including Thomas White, Peter Lombard, and Nicholas and Patrick Comerford. Richard was in no doubt about his debt to White and to his parents for sending him to Kilkenny: 'it was my happy happe (God and my parents be thanked) to have been one of his crew', to the extent that 'I reverence the meanest stone cemented in the walls of that famous school in Kilkenny'.[5]

Besides his dedication to the advancing of educational standards in Ireland, James had a strong commitment to codifying and printing the statutes passed in Irish parliaments over the previous several centuries. Not only did he have a humanist's zeal to preserve and disseminate older documents, but he also saw in the publishing of the statutory basis of English rule in Ireland a way of defending the patrimony of the English community. We have seen that he had some bundles of statutes in his home that were used by Campion in compiling his history, and other officials had their own collections. In 1571 a collation was made of 170 acts of the Irish parliament passed from the fifteenth century down to 1571, and a committee of the Irish judges examined and edited them. In August 1571 James Stanihurst was deputed to bring the full transcript of the statutes and laws to England, and was granted expenses of £59 for his travel and sojourn at the press. In letters that he bore to court, Stanihurst was commended for his initiative in furthering the project. When the text of the statutes was printed in London at the press of Richard Tottell in 1572, there was available in Ireland and England for the first time a systematic guide to statutory law both for government officials and agents, and for the older English community, who regarded the body of legislation as the bedrock of their constitution.

That that constitution was under threat from ambitious English newcomers had been evident for some time by the early 1570s. The changing religious regimes affected the balance between papacy, crown and community that had framed the English settlement in Ireland since the twelfth century. Reluctance on the part of most of the older English community to embrace doctrinal reform was adumbrated in the 1560 parliamentary proceedings. Then, in the parliament of 1569–71 at which

James Stanihurst was again in position in the speaker's chair, there were bitter clashes between the representatives of the older English interest and vocal newcomers over land and privileges. Reform of religion and education was overshadowed by a new colonial mentality on the part of some of these recent arrivals, who tended to disdain the older English as provincial and conservative, especially in respect of their confessional views. While Sir Henry Sidney was chief governor, he tried to strike a balance between the factions, but on his recall to England in 1571 the native reformers of the English Pale were lacking a champion. Among these was James Stanihurst, who had relied upon the patronage of Sidney for his preferment in his later years. As a consequence of Sidney's departure from Dublin, Edmund Campion, whom Sidney patronized, now felt insecure and fled from the city. He went first to Turvey House, the home of Sir Christopher Barnewall, and ultimately left Ireland altogether to seek refuge on the Continent. It was while he sheltered at Turvey that Campion completed the manuscript of his *Histories of Ireland*.

Towards the end of his comparatively brief life, there is evidence that James Stanihurst was finding it difficult to gain a positive response from the English court to his petitions for preferment. Perhaps his career was also affected by the removal of Sir Henry Sidney, who had acted as his patron. Many of James' leases of properties, granted in the 1540s and 1550s, were falling due for renewal in 1572, including the monastery of Odder as well as other farms in town and countryside. He was also experiencing a delay in receiving recompense for his journey to London with the statutes. At this time James had proposed the resuscitation of the office of escheator general, which one of his ancestors had held in the late Middle Ages. The escheator had responsibility for testing the title to lands, the tenant-in-chief of which had died, and conveying them back to crown ownership, if such a transfer were justified. Stanihurst made a case for the revival of the escheatorship on the basis that the queen was losing her rights to many properties through the lack of such an office. There was reluctance on the part of some in the administration in Dublin to recommend Stanihurst, certainly as exclusive holder of the office. We have seen that Archbishop Loftus of Dublin had reservations about James' religious stance and he proposed that he be joined in the escheatorship by an Englishman, Robert Powesley, whom he perceived to be a man of 'godliness and true religion'.[6] Queen Elizabeth eventually agreed to the suggestion of a joint tenure between Stanihurst and the English-born official.

James did not live very much longer to enjoy the fruits of his offices. He died on 27 December 1573. A commemorative sonnet in Latin, composed by his son in his honour, contained the following tribute:

> The city has lost a wise man, the courts a guiding light,
> The client has lost an advocate, and the young man a father.

James' death not only brought an end to the most successful career of a Stanihurst in public life to date, but also it represented the end of an era. None of his descendants attained public office thereafter, his eldest son, Richard, becoming a schoolmaster and later a scholar in exile. While there is no evidence for the Stanihurst family legal tradition continuing beyond James' generation, education in the law did remain a popular career path for youngsters from the Pale. Gradually, however, most of the higher judicial offices were conferred on newly arrived Englishmen.

The reputation of members of the legal profession was quite high at the end of the medieval period. In Chaucer's *Canterbury Tales*, for example, the man of law was portrayed as 'ware and wise', 'discreet', 'full rich of excellence' and 'of great reverence' (pl. 16). Although somewhat self-important and not quite so busy as he made himself out to be, there was no doubt about his professional expertise. James Stanihurst fits very well the mould of public-spirited and dedicated lawyer. While prospering through his practice and advancing himself socially, James was described as honest and wise. His commitment to the reform of his country and its inhabitants was expressed in his speeches and he himself set an example by his dedication to public service, his patronage of pedagogy and his zeal for the dissemination of knowledge of the constitution and history. He was faced with a dilemma as to his religious profession, but died before he was forced to declare himself openly. Above all, he was a humanistic reformer who resisted confessional ideology and, instead, believed in the efficacy of learning and education to promote moral and social improvement.

The Poet's Tale

KATHARINE SIMMS

Before I begin the tale of Maoilín Óg Mac Bruaideadha, it is perhaps best to give a brief overview of who the bardic poets were, how much interaction they had with the English-speaking inhabitants of the larger towns in medieval Ireland and what I mean by the phrase 'bardic poetry'. The word 'bard' occurs in various forms in all societies of Celtic origin – Gaulish, Welsh and Scottish as well as Irish – but when used by Irish language scholars like Eleanor Knott or Osborn Bergin the phrase applies very specifically to early modern Irish syllabic poetry composed in Ireland and Scotland between the thirteenth and the seventeenth century, what is normally called in Modern Irish *filíocht na scol*, the 'poetry of the schools'.[1]

The internal evidence of the poems themselves shows a society in which professional bardic poetry was practised at two levels, for the aristocracy and for the general public. All professional poets were entertainers – they gave public performances for material reward wherever an audience was gathered – in banqueting halls where a chieftain or lord was holding a feast for invited guests, whether this was a Christmas feast, a royal inauguration, a wedding, a funeral or a feast following a year's mind memorial mass. They also came to the green in front of a lord's castle, or to traditional gathering-hills on days when the lord's vassals and humbler subjects assembled once or twice a year for the *aonach ⁊ ardoireachtas*, the territorial council where cases were judged, taxes were proclaimed, debates over peace and war were held, and where a lot of trading, begging and match-making took place on the fringes. There are references to bands of poets shouting to draw attention to their performance on such occasions.[2] Not surprisingly, those who could afford it employed a professional reciter and a musical accompanist.

The most prestigious companies of poets that might visit a chieftain's court were those led by an *ollamh*, a term that could imply the court poet attached to a particular chieftain, rewarded for his services with a plot of land and an annual pension of cows, but also described the head of a hereditary family of poets, the master of a poetic school of apprentices and pupils in the poetic art. The same man could occupy all three roles, and being an official court poet to one chieftain did not preclude a poet from going on tour, making a *cuairt* or passing visit to the courts of other patrons. On the other hand, a chieftain might be blessed or cursed with having several hereditary families of local poets holding land in his vicinity, and he would have to select only one man from these possible candidates to be his official court poet, or indeed he could decide to employ a talented outsider who had impressed him with his skill while on *cuairt*, a poetic visit to the chief's court (fig. 14.1).[3]

Text-books from the poetic schools and the commentaries that accompany them indicate that educated poets in the High Middle Ages could be recruited from various backgrounds. The most obvious route was to be the son of a professional poet, particularly if the father was an *ollamh* at the head of his profession, master of a bardic school and endowed with an estate of tax-free lands that he hoped to pass on to his son. But the members of other learned professions – the historians or genealogists, the brehon lawyers and the native physicians – also learned to read and write in Irish at their schools and to compose Irish verse, and sometimes members of these families decided to undergo the full training as a professional praise poet. In addition, Irish clerics, and even tenants living on church lands, who were often descended from the early Irish monastic families, learned to read, write and versify in Irish and so a number of fully qualified praise-poets came from an ecclesiastical background.[4]

The Mac Bruaideadha family illustrates these connections perfectly. In the historical records we find three branches of the family living in Co. Clare, all related to one another, although the exact links are unclear. One branch were learned ecclesiasts: their head was hereditary keeper of the shrine of St Caimin of Inishcealtra on the shores of Lough Derg and he

14.1 'MacSweeney's Feast', pl. 3, from John Derricke's, *The image of Ireland*, 1581.

possessed a fine library of ecclesiastical manuscripts. A second branch specialized as court poets to the O'Brien chieftains of Thomond – Daire and his two sons, Domhnall mac Daire and Tadhg mac Daire. Tadhg lived at Knockanalban or Mount Scott, near to the O'Brien chief seat at Ennis, although he also held land as a tenant of the bishop of Killaloe. The third branch were hereditary *ollamhs* of history and poetry to the territories of Uí Breacáin and Cinéal Fermaic near Miltown Malbay and they ran a bardic school at Lettermoylan on the slopes of Mount Callan. It was to this branch that Maoilín Óg belonged. His father and his two uncles had in turn succeeded to the title of chief of this learned family and head of the school of history and poetry at Lettermoylan. His father had risen above merely local importance to become known as *ollamh* in history to Conor O'Brien, third earl of Thomond. The next earl, Donough O'Brien, had been fostered as a young child by the sister of Tadhg mac Daire Mac Bruaideadha, and Tadhg mac Daire achieved life-long status as court poet and historian to the fourth earl of Thomond, leaving Maoilín Óg to become head of the family and of the Mount Callan school in succession to his uncle Giolla Brighde sometime before 1599.[5]

Dublin was the last place in Ireland you would expect to meet a bardic poet. The inhabitants, especially those in the upper classes, were normally monoglot English speakers and quite hostile to the Irish language and Irish culture. Richard Stanihurst, a Dubliner himself, deplored the fact that Irish was beginning to spread in the late sixteenth century into the surrounding area of the Pale. As he said,

> put the case that the Irishe tongue were as sacred as the Hebrewe, as learned as the Greeke, as fluent as the Latin, as amorous as the Italian, as courteous as the Hispanish, as courtelike as the French, yet truly… I see not, but it may be very well spared in the Englishe pale … One demanded meryly, why *O Neale*, that last was, would not frame himselfe to speake English? 'What', quoth the other, in a rage, 'thinkest thou, that it standeth with *O Neale* his honor to wryeth his mouth in clattering Englishe?' And yet forsooth we must gagge our iawes in gybbrishing Irish![6]

Limerick was different, since it was in closer contact with its Irish hinterland. We have a jolly tale in late Middle Irish about a student poet from Co. Clare who sent his servants into Limerick to sell cattle and buy a luxury present for his fiancée, a rich woman from Corcovaskin. One of the servants picked a fight with a Limerick man and was arrested. The poet went to see the foreign governor of the town, whether this was a Viking jarl or an English mayor, and threatened to satirize the inhabitants unless his servant was released, but he was told that poetic sanctions had no force among the foreigners. So the trainee poet went off to a school of bardic poets in Clare and gathered a band of the students to come back with him to Limerick and seize two horses in revenge. The men of Limerick then arrested the innocent son of the head teacher of the bardic school, who happened to be in town at the time, and held him as security for the return of the mares. The students defied their teacher's pleas, ran off with the horses, and he was left to foot the bill for his son's ransom himself. The tale ends with a bitter poem by the teacher, saying 'Never again will I trust a student'.[7] From about 1375 we also have a poem attributed to a well-known poet Aodh Mór Mag Craith of Tipperary satirizing a mayor of Limerick, Sir Thomas Clifford, who is compared to his disadvantage with the local chief, Mac Í Bhriain Ara:

> A bumpy forehead in a small face, the sure signs of an idiot; he has provoked the derision of the assembly on account of his mottled pate.
>
> His eyebrows standing up in tufts over his two pupils, these are not serene eyes but are set in cold wet sockets...
>
> The drip of his crooked nose – certainly there is here the very pattern of ugliness – every secretion from his nostrils is an undrinkable cliff-stream![8] (and so it goes on!)

We know, however, that poets did come to Dublin on various occasions. Like the student poet who hoped to buy an engagement present in Limerick, they might come to do their shopping. A *crosántacht* poem, which intersperses verses of praise with prose anecdotes, to Feidhlim son of Fiach mac Hugh O'Byrne tells a comic tale of a band of poets who came to Dublin to buy weapons and armour, and the merchant asked them to sell him a poem for £10, planning to re-sell it to the famously generous O'Conor of Sligo for £20. So ignorant was the Dublin man of Irish poetry and traditions, he did not realize that for a chief to buy a poem it was supposed to be in praise of himself or his ancestors, and the poets cynically sold him an old poem that had nothing to do with O'Conor. The story goes on to say that O'Conor of Sligo was so extravagantly generous that, when he heard how the poets had cheated the merchant, he paid him £20 pounds anyway for his worthless text.[9]

A more drastic reason for a poet to come to Dublin is also found in the O'Byrne poem-book. A court poet was duty-bound to recite an elegy over the body of his dead patron, but when that patron had been captured and executed by the Dublin government, and the head and/or dismembered body parts displayed over the gates of the city, the poet came to stand outside the walls and recite his elegy there, as in the case of Fiach mac Hugh

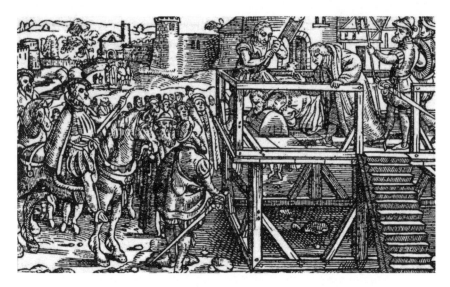

14.2 Execution of a traitor from Stanihurst's 'Description of Ireland' in Holinshed's *Chronicles*, 1577 edition (© Huntington Library).

O'Byrne himself in 1597. Fiach's personal poet Domhnall Mac Eochadha may have been first on the spot, since he seems to have had a sight of Fiach's decapitated head before it was shipped to England for public display in London. In his poem *Mairg do-chonnarc ceann Fhiachaidh*, 'Woe to him who saw Fiacha's head', he laments 'Woe to the foot that brought me to Dublin to the place where I saw him in quarters, woe to the eyelid that opened and forced me to see the stately head and the noble fragrant body lifeless and motionless'.[10] A second poet, Aonghas Ó Dálaigh, perhaps arriving somewhat later, mourned *A cholann do-chím gan ceann*, 'O body I see without a head, The four limbs I saw in Dublin, divided up between the four stakes, have blinded my heart with woe' (fig. 14.2).[11]

Another group with bardic associations who would have been obliged to visit Dublin from time to time were the native Irish medical men, coming to buy the raw materials for their medicines. An English chemist, Thomas Smyth, set up shop in Dublin and in 1561 he wrote a detailed description of the bardic professions. He describes the brehon lawyers, the historians or shanachies, and the poets, the Aos Dána, with the hangers-on who accompanied them to the feasts and fairs, the musicians, reciters, jugglers, gamesters and 'the Gogathe, which is to say in English, the glutayne, for one of them will eate 2 or 3 galons of butter at a sitinge, halfe a mutton'.[12] Significantly, he omitted reference to the native doctors. Possibly this newcomer from England gleaned his surprisingly detailed information on Irish learned classes from conversations with bardic medical men coming as customers. In a curious passage that has no parallels among other descriptions of the Irish poetic class, he distinguishes between ordinary praise poets, the *Aos Dána*, and the *file* or learned poet:

> The fourth sort of Rymers is called Fillis, which is to say in English, a Poete. Theis men have great store of cattell, and use all the trades of the others, with an adicion of prophecies. Theis are great mayntayners of whitches and other vile matters; to the great blasfemye of God and to the great impoverishinge of the comenwealthe.[13]

His remarks carry a special interest in relation to Maoilín Óg Mac Bruaideadha, the bardic teacher from Clare. Whereas the Irish annals, when recording the death of court poets in the period after the Norman invasion, normally describe them as *fir dána* ('men with the gift of poetry'), in other words members of the *Aos Dána* as described by Thomas Smyth, it is said of Maoilín Óg in his death notice under the year 1602: *Ní bhaoi i nÉrinn i n-én pearsain seanchaidh, file agus fear dána do bferr inás*, 'There was not in Ireland, in the person of one individual, a better historian, poet and rhymer, than he'.[14]

There are at least three reasons why Maoilín Óg should be singled out by the compilers of the Annals of the Four Masters for this write-up and for the title *file* or learned poet. In the first place, just as Thomas Smyth states that the *file* 'used all the trades', Maolín Óg combined two professions as a historian and a fully qualified poet, and he taught both subjects in his school at Lettermoylan. Thus, he was indeed a 'learned poet'. Secondly, the Ó Cléirigh family, to which most of the Four Masters team of compilers belonged, were related by marriage to Maoilín Óg. In the middle of the sixteenth century the Ó Cléirigh poets got into a dispute with the Ó Gallachair family, who had violated a safe-conduct under their poetic guarantee, and they were forced out of their Donegal lands to seek refuge in Co. Clare. There Mac Con Ó Cléirigh met and intermarried with the learned family of Mac Bruaideadha. The biographer of Red Hugh O'Donnell, Lughaidh son of Mac Con Ó Cléirigh, was thus a kinsman of Tadhg Mac Daire Mheic Bhruaideadha, a relationship that caused comment during the Contention of the Bards, 'an erudite poetic dispute that broke out about 1616, as to whether the northern or southern dynasties were best entitled to the high-kingship'.[15] The third and most likely reason for the high praise in Maoilín Óg's obituary is found in the preface to the Four Masters' annals, where they explain that one of the sources they were using was the annals of Maoilín Óg Mac Bruaideadha, for the years 1588 to 1603.[16] Since Maoilín Óg himself died in 1602, this set of annals was continued for a short time after the historian's death, presumably in his school of Lettermoylan, whose direction passed first to Tadhg Mac Daire Mheic Bhruaideadha and later to Maoilín Óg's own son, Conchobhar Mac Bruaideadha. In such an environment, this set of annals would naturally close with a complimentary notice on their original compiler.

It may well be from Maoilín Óg's annals that the Four Masters obtained a very detailed description of an incident that took place in Dublin in 1597:

> One hundred and forty-four barrels of powder were sent by the queen to Dublin, to her people, in the month of March. When the powder was landed, it was drawn to Wine-street [no. 25 on Speed's map above, p. ii], and placed on both sides of the street, and a spark of fire got into the powder; but from whence that spark proceeded, whether from the heavens or from the earth beneath, is not known; howbeit, the barrels burst into one blazing flame and rapid conflagration [13 March], which raised into the air, from their solid foundations and supporting posts, the stone mansions and wooden houses of the street, so that the long beam, the enormous stone, and

the man in his corporal shape, were sent whirling into the air over the town by the explosion of this powerful powder; and it is impossible to enumerate, reckon or describe the number of honourable persons, of tradesmen of every class, of women and maidens, and of the sons of gentlemen, who had come from all parts of Ireland to be educated in the city, that were destroyed. The quantity of gold, silver or worldly property that was destroyed, was no cause of lamentation, compared to the number of people who were injured and killed by that explosion. It was not Wine-street alone that was destroyed on this occasion, but the next quarter of the town to it.[17]

The reference to 'sons of gentlemen' who had come to Dublin from all parts of Ireland to be educated reminds us not only that Trinity College had been founded five years earlier in 1592, but that Maoilín Óg himself is described as being based there in the year of his death, 1602. He may already have come to Dublin before the time of the explosion, since he was contributing to an Irish translation of the New Testament, which was proposed in 1596 to be printed at the college's printing press and the printer to be paid by a grant from the college.[18] If the sons of gentlemen who were blown up in Winetavern Street were indeed students from Trinity, they were out of bounds, since an early record of disciplinary action taken against delinquent students in the college lists among their offences lodging in town, and resorting to ale-houses, an offence punished by beating with a rod. Other offences included playing at cards in the porter's lodging in the steeple, climbing the college walls and breaking the provost's windows.[19]

His Protestant O'Brien patrons no doubt recommended Maoilín Óg's services on the New Testament project because of his general expertise in Irish literary style. Although Maoilín Óg was a very competent composer of *dán díreach* verse, which was the strict rhyming mode of composition used by professional praise poets, almost all the poems we have from him today are historical and genealogical in content, and this combined with his authorship of a set of annals suggests that his main vocation was as a historian rather than as a poet. One of his best-known compositions is an address to the O'Brien castle at Ennis, listing all the chieftains who occupied it since it was first built.[20]

Another more enigmatic poem, *Bráthair do'n bhás an doidhbhreas*, 'Poverty is brother to Death', is attributed to Maoilín Óg Mac Bruaideadha in a nineteenth-century copy by the scribe Mícheál Óg Ó Longáin, and was clearly composed in the O'Brien lordship during the reign of Queen Elizabeth (1558–1603). It is written in the looser style of rhyming, *óglachas*, used for informal or amateur compositions. The author has just lost his employment with an O'Brien leader whom he describes as 'chieftain of the River Fergus'. This man was identified by Thomas O'Rahilly as Conor O'Brien, third earl of Thomond,[21] who earned the condemnation of the bardic schools of Ireland by hanging three poets in 1572, before eventually dying in 1580 and leaving an underage son, Donough, fourth earl of Thomond, as his heir.[22] Another O'Brien who would fit the description equally well was Sir Turlough O'Brien of Dough Castle near Lahinch, ancestor of the Ennistymon branch, a patron who was addressed by Maoilín Óg in a long genealogical poem, *Cuirfead comaoin ar Chloinn Táil*, 'I will confer a favour on the descendants of Tál (that is, the O'Briens)', the first of Maoilín Óg's major works to be listed by the Four Masters in his obituary. Sir Turlough lived much closer to Maoilín Óg's own base at Mount Callan and Lettermoylan and shared Earl Conor O'Brien's characteristics of Protestantism and cooperation with the English government.[23] In *Bráthair do'n bhás an doidhbhreas*, the angry poet threatens to take revenge for his dismissal by informing the English government that his erstwhile patron is generous, honours those who avoid taxes, reverences holy wells and statues, is kind to enemies and patronizes bardic poetry. He ends by hoping for a renewal of patronage. Since he has just lost his job as poet, and the O'Brien in question, whether the third earl or Sir Turlough, was a Protestant, these threats to inform on him are likely to have been sarcastic. Highlighting his former patron's heresy, stinginess and vengeful nature, but yet also emphasizing characteristics that would form the basis of a praise-poem for any other chief, he left the door open for reconciliation. Though we cannot be certain that the poem *Bráthair do'n bhás an doidhbhreas* was actually the work of Maoilín Óg, it highlights the difficulty facing a bardic poet who was a Catholic nationalist if his local patrons were Protestant loyalists.

We have a stronger reason to suppose that Maoilín Óg was sympathetic to the nationalist side in the Nine Years War – the rebellion led by Red Hugh O'Donnell and Hugh O'Neill, earl of Tyrone, 1594–1603 – from an incident that took place in 1599. At that time the army of Red Hugh O'Donnell, on its way southwards, plundered the O'Brien territories in Co. Clare and seized cattle from the lands of both Maoilín Óg and his kinsman Tadhg Mac Daire Mheic Bhruaideadha. Tadhg mac Dáire responded with a savage poem cursing O'Donnell, threatening him with defeat in battle and a short life unless he restored the plunder,[24] prophecies that soon came true with the disastrous Battle of Kinsale and Red Hugh's death in Spain shortly thereafter. Maoilín Óg by contrast travelled to O'Donnell's camp and recited a poem in his honour in which he stated that Red Hugh was the prophesied deliverer of Ireland and that the plunder of Co. Clare was a just revenge for the demolition of the fort of Aileach on Inishowen by the high-king Muircheartach O'Brien in 1101. We have only one verse of this poem preserved in the Annals of the Four Masters,[25] perhaps originally recorded in Maoilín Óg's own set of annals, but we can see from this one verse that the poem was in highly ornamented strict metre, in the mode known as *séadhna*. In contrast to Tadhg mac Daire, Maoilín Óg's cattle were returned to him by O'Donnell in payment for his poem. The other details of this incident make clear that Maoilín Óg, if he ever was the angry unemployed poet who wrote *Bráthair do'n bhás an daidhbhreas*, had now progressed to a person of considerable wealth and reputation. In 1599 he was head of his branch of the Mac Bruaideadha family and master of the bardic school on Mount Callan, evidently respected by both his immediate patrons the Protestant O'Briens and the nationalist O'Donnells.

Exactly when he moved to Dublin is unclear, but it could have been soon after his encounter with Red Hugh since the rebel army continued to ravage Munster throughout 1599 and 1600. Trinity College had been founded in 1592 on the grounds of the dissolved priory of All Hallows, outside what were then the walls of Dublin. Maoilín Óg took up his residence there, apparently as a consulting editor along with another bardic poet, Domhnall Óg Ó hUiginn. They were editing an ongoing project of Uilliam Ó Domhnaill, one of the first fellows of Trinity College and later Protestant archbishop of Tuam, who was translating the Greek New Testament into Irish. This work was eventually published in 1602–3, the preface being written just before Maoilín Óg died. In this, Archbishop Ó Domhnaill acknowledges the assistance of Maoilín Óg, referring to him as *Duine iúlmhar sa teanguidh Ghaoidheilge sa choláiste nuadh láimh ré Baile Átha Cliath,* 'a person knowledgeable in the Irish tongue, in the new college beside Dublin'.[26] Maoilín Óg died that year on 31 December and it seems quite probable that he died in Trinity College, although he is likely to have been buried with his ancestors in Clare.

It is notable that the Four Masters, who noted the exact day of his death, said nothing about where he was at the time and, while they include in the death-notice a list of his most famous poetic compositions, they are silent about his role in helping the Protestant Ó Domhnaill to translate the New Testament, probably because they disapproved (fig. 14.3). Yet the Four Masters themselves were subsidized during their work on the annals by the chieftain Fearghal O'Gara, who had been in his day a student at Trinity College.[27] It is an interesting fact that when it came to the pursuit of higher learning, whether in the search for manuscripts of the Latin lives of Irish saints,[28] or historical annals and poems in Irish,[29] there actually was cooperation between scholars of the Counter-Reformation and those Protestants, mostly of Old English extraction, who took an interest in Irish history and literature. Both Tadhg mac Daire and his kinsman Maoilín Óg Mac Bruaideadha were clearly under pressure from their O'Brien patrons to conform to the Anglican church and during the Contention of the Bards the Franciscan poet, Roibéard Mac Artúir, made insinuations against Tadhg mac Daire's continuance in Catholic orthodoxy.[30] Interestingly, Tadhg mac Daire's religious poetry[31] could be described as non-denominational, centred on basic Christian themes common to both traditions and avoiding any points of controversy. What little we know or can guess about Maoilín

TIOMNA NVADH

AR DTIGHEARNA AGVS

AR SLANAIGHTHEORA IOSA
CRIOSD,

AR NA TARRUING GU FIRINNEACH
ar Ġreigir gu gaoioheilg,

RE HUILLIAM O DOMHNUILL

·Tit. Cap. 2.

Uerr. 11. Do foilligh grás De gu teallmuigteach, do beir rlánughadh rir do chum na nuile dáoineadh:

Uerr. 13. Agus do beir teaguyg dúine, rá neam! dįághacho, agus rá airmiánuib an tráoghailye ċo ṛeachna, agus ri an mbeatha olio chaiteam ohúiń gu meararrġa, agus gu conicrom, agus gu oıaġá, ra ráoghalra to lathair.

ATA SO AR NA CHUR AGCLO AMBAILE
athá Cliath, a otigh mhaiżiptiʁ Uilliam Uiréiʁ Chois an Opuich-tio, ré Seón Ffrancke. 1602.

14.3 Cover of seventeenth-century Irish translation of New Testament, from E.R.McC. Dix and J.T. Gilbert, 'Irish bibliography: two papers by the late Sir John T. Gilbert', *PRIA*, 25C (1904–5), 117–42 at 136 (by permission of the Royal Irish Academy © RIA).

Óg suggests that he was more decidedly Catholic and nationalist, but in matters of pure scholarship he took no sides and in this he seems to have been typical of a number of educated Irishmen in the late sixteenth century. It is because such men managed to interest even some of the newly arrived planters in the learning of the bardic schools that we have a store of medieval Irish manuscripts not only in Trinity itself and later the Royal Irish Academy, but also in the Bodleian Library in Oxford.[32] Maoilín Óg Mac Bruaideadha, who combined the role of hereditary bardic poet and genealogist with that of proof-reader for the Irish printing-press at Trinity College, who praised the rebels in the Nine Years War and yet helped with the Protestant translation of the New Testament in Dublin, is in his own person an archetype of the transitions taking place around 1600 between the Ireland of the Middle Ages and that of the early modern period. At the same time he was one of an important group of scholars who bridged the cultural gap and transmitted the learning of the past into our modern world.

Endnotes

꧁꧂

Introduction and acknowledgments

[1] For more detail on the foundation of the FMD, see H.B. Clarke, 'Thirty years on: a personal memoir of the Friends of Medieval Dublin' in S. Duffy (ed.), *Medieval Dublin VIII* (Dublin, 2008), pp 318–28.

The Saint's Tale

[1] See L. Simpson, 'Fifty years a-digging: a synthesis of medieval archaeological investigations in Dublin city and suburbs' in S. Duffy (ed.), *Medieval Dublin XI* (Dublin, 2011), pp 9–112 at pp 21–2.

[2] See M. Gowen, 'Excavations at the site of the church and tower of St Michael le Pole, Dublin' in S. Duffy (ed.), *Medieval Dublin II* (Dublin, 2001), pp 13–52; E. O'Donovan, 'The Irish, the Vikings and the English: new archaeological evidence from excavations at Golden Lane, Dublin' in S. Duffy (ed.), *Medieval Dublin VIII* (Dublin, 2008), pp 36–130.

[3] See *Rerum Hibernicarum scriptores, Tom III; Complectens annales IV magistrorum, ex ipso O'Clerii autographo in Bibliotheca Stowense*, ed. C. O'Conor (Buckingham, 1826), p. 212; *AFM*, i, pp 264–5; RIA MS C iii 3, fo. 256r; RIA MS 23 F 2, fo. 63.

[4] I am grateful to Dr Cunningham for sharing her opinion on this matter. For discussion of the scribal team, see her *The Annals of the Four Masters: Irish history, kingship and society in the early seventeenth century* (Dublin, 2010), chap. 6.

[5] *MD*.

[6] P. Ó Riain, *Feastdays of the saints: a history of Irish martyrologies* (Brussels, 2006), pp 281–313.

[7] Dubhaltach Mac Fhirbhisigh, *Leabhar Genealach. The Great Book of Irish Genealogies*, ed. N. Ó Muraíle (Dublin, 2003–4); see also idem, *The celebrated antiquary Dubhaltach Mac Fhirbhisigh, c.1600–1671: his lineage, life and learning* (Maynooth, 1996).

[8] N. Ó Muraíle, 'The manuscripts of the Annals of the Four Masters since 1636' in E. Bhreathnach and B. Cunningham (eds), *Writing Irish history: the Four Masters and their world* (Dublin, 2007), pp 60–7 at p. 61.

[9] R. O'Flaherty, *Ogygia: seu, rerum Hibernicarum chronologia* (London, 1685); on

him, see R. Sharpe, *Roderick O'Flaherty's letters to William Molyneux, Edward Lhwyd, and Samuel Molyneux, 1696–1709* (Dublin, 2013).

¹⁰ N. Ó Muraíle, 'The role of Charles O'Conor of Belanagare in the Irish manuscript tradition' in P. Ó Macháin (ed.), *The Book of the O'Conor Don: essays on an Irish manuscript* (Dublin, 2010), pp 226–44.

¹¹ C. O'Conor, *Dissertations on the antient history of Ireland, wherein an account is given of the origine, government, letters, sciences, manners and customs, of the antient inhabitants* (Dublin, 1748 (in separate parts); 1753 (book form)).

¹² See, for example, R.A. Breatnach, 'The end of a tradition: a survey of eighteenth-century Gaelic literature', *Studia Hibernica*, 1 (1961), 128–38; N. Ní Shéaghdha, 'Irish scholars and scribes in eighteenth-century Dublin', *Eighteenth-Century Ireland*, 4 (1989), 41–54; D. Ó Catháin, 'Charles O'Conor of Belanagare: antiquary and Irish scholar', *JRSAI*, 119 (1989), 136–63.

¹³ C.A. Sheehan, 'The O'Conor manuscripts in the Stowe Ashburnham collection', *Studies*, 41 (1952), 362–9.

¹⁴ *Annales IV magistrorum, ex ipso O'Clerii autographo in Bibliotheca Stowense*, ed. C. O'Conor, in *Rerum Hibernicarum scriptores*, vol. III (Buckingham, 1826).

¹⁵ D. Ó Catháin, 'John Fergus MD, eighteenth-century doctor, book collector and Irish scholar', *JRSAI*, 118 (1988), 139–62.

¹⁶ Ó Catháin, 'Charles O'Conor of Belanagare', 146; W. O'Sullivan, 'The Irish manuscripts in Case H in Trinity College Dublin', *Celtica*, 11 (1976), 229–50, at 231–2; R.B. McDowell and D.A. Webb, *Trinity College Dublin 1592–1952: an academic history* (1982), pp 50, 65; C. Coogan Ward and R.E. Ward (eds), *The letters of Charles O'Conor of Belanagare*, i: *1731–71* (Ann Arbor, MI, 1980), pp 164–5.

¹⁷ *RIA cat. Ir. MSS*, facs. XXII, ed. K. Mulchrone (Dublin, 1937), no. 988, pp 987–8.

¹⁸ Ó Muraíle, 'The role of Charles O'Conor of Belanagare in the Irish manuscript tradition', pp 232–4. I am very grateful to Dr Ó Muraíle for bringing his identification to my attention.

¹⁹ Ward and Ward (eds), *Letters of Charles O'Conor*, nos 341, 343, 344, 364, 370.

²⁰ B. Mac Giolla Phádraig, 'Dr John Carpenter, archbishop of Dublin, 1770–1786', *Dublin Historical Record*, 30:1 (1976), 2–17.

²¹ For which, see for example, M.H. Risk, 'Seán Ó Neachtain', *Studia Hibernica*, 15 (1975), 47–60; Ní Shéaghdha, 'Irish scholars and scribes in eighteenth-century Dublin'; C. Ó Háinle, 'A life in eighteenth-century Dublin: Tadhg Ó Neachtain' in V. Uibh Eachach (ed.), *Feile Zozimus: 18th and 19th Century Dublin* (Dublin, 1991), pp 10–28.

22 RIA MS 23 A 8, fol. x; I am very grateful to Professor Ó Riain for bringing the manuscript to my attention.

23 C. Etchingham, 'Bishops in the early Irish church: a reassessment', *Studia Hibernica*, 28 (1994), 35–62 at 49.

24 Ibid.; W. Davies, 'Clerics as rulers: some implications of the terminology of ecclesiastical authority in early medieval Ireland' in N.P. Brooks (ed.), *Latin and the vernacular languages in early medieval Britain* (Leicester, 1982), pp 84–5.

25 *AU*, pp 118–19 *s.a.* 635.

26 *AFM*, i, pp 250–1, *s.a.* 630=635; T.M. Charles-Edwards, *Early Christian Ireland* (Cambridge, 2000), p. 250.

27 P. Ó Riain, *A dictionary of Irish saints* (Dublin, 2011), p. 473.

28 But cf. Ó Riain, *Dictionary of Irish saints*, pp 292, 453.

29 But cf. www.gaelicplacenames.org/databasedetails.php?id=123; I am grateful to Drs M. Cotter and J. King of *Ainmean-Àite na h-Alba* for their assistance.

30 Ó Riain, *Dictionary of Irish saints*, pp 94–6.

31 Ibid., p. 96.

32 Ó Riain, *Feastdays of the saints: a history of Irish martyrologies*, p. 301.

33 *MD*, pp 120–1; cf. Ó Riain, *Dictionary of Irish saints*, p. 580.

34 John Colgan, *Triadis Thaumaturgæ seu divorum Patricii, Columbæ et Brigidæ, trium veteris et maioris Scotiæ, seu Hiberniæ sanctorum insulae communium patronorum acta* (Louvain, 1647), p. 112, n. 69.

35 'A Catholicke priest' [John Wilson], *The English martyrologe conteyning a summary of the liues of the glorious and renowned saintes of the three kingdomes, England, Scotland, and Ireland* (Saint-Omer, 1608), p. 152.

36 Jan Vermeulen, *Indiculus sanctorum Belgii, auctore Ioanne Molano Lovaniensi, sacrarum literarum Lovanii regio porofessore* (Louvain, 1572), p. 68.

37 Sir James Ware, *De praesulibus Hiberniae commentarius a prima gentis Hibernicae ad fidem Christianam conversione, ad nostra usque tempora* (Dublin, 1665), p. 101.

38 W. Harris (ed.), *The works of Sir James Ware concerning Ireland revised and improved. In three volumes. Vol. I. Containing, the history of the bishops ... Vol. II. Containing, the antiquities of Ireland. Vol. III. Containing, the writers of Ireland. In two books. All written in Latin ... now newly translated into English* (3 vols, Dublin, 1739–46), i, pp 303–4.

39 Laurientius Surius, *De probatis sanctorum vitis quas tam ex MSS codicibus quam ex editis authoribus: Maivs* (Cologne, 1618), pp 98–9.

40 Vermeulen, *Indiculus sanctorum Belgii*, p. 84.

[41] *MD*, pp 120–1.

[42] RIA MS 23 A 8, fo. x.

[43] Surius, *De probatis sanctorum vitis*, pp 98–9.

[44] RIA MS C iii 3, fo. 256r.

The Skeleton's Tale

[1] The writer, acting for the former Margaret Gowen and Co. Ltd, directed the excavation, which was carried out on behalf of Dunnes Stores in December 2003 (licence 99E0414).

[2] L. Simpson, 'Viking warrior burials in Dublin: is this the *longphort*?' in S. Duffy (ed.), *Medieval Dublin VI* (Dublin, 2005), pp 11–62.

[3] L. Simpson, 'Fifty years a-digging: a synthesis of medieval archaeological investigations in Dublin city and the suburbs' in S. Duffy (ed.), *Medieval Dublin XI* (Dublin, 2011), pp 9–112.

[4] S. Harrison, 'Bride Street revisited: Viking burial in Dublin and beyond' in S. Duffy (ed.), *Medieval Dublin X* (Dublin, 2010), pp 126–52 at p. 127.

[5] A. MacShamhráin, *The Vikings: an illustrated history* (Dublin, 2002); S. Duffy, *Brian Boru and the Battle of Clontarf* (Dublin, 2013).

[6] R. Ó Floinn, 'The archaeology of the early Viking Age in Ireland' in H.B. Clarke, M. Ní Mhaonaigh and R. Ó Floinn (eds), *Ireland and Scandinavia in the early Viking Age* (Dublin, 1998), pp 132–65.

[7] E. O'Donovan, 'The Irish, the Vikings and the English: new archaeological evidence from excavations at Golden Lane, Dublin' in S. Duffy (ed.), *Medieval Dublin VIII* (Dublin, 2008), pp 36–130.

[8] M. Biddle and B. Kjolbye-Biddle, 'Repton and the Vikings', *Antiquity*, 66 (1992), 36–51 at 41.

[9] C. Downham, 'Viking camps in ninth-century Ireland: sources, locations and interactions' in S. Duffy (ed.), *Medieval Dublin XI* (Dublin, 2010), pp 93–125 at p. 117.

The Slave's Tale

[1] O. Holder-Egger (ed.), *Monumenta Germaniae historica: scriptores rerum Germanicarum* (Hanover, 1887; repr. 1992), xv, pp 502–6. The Latin text and an English translation by K. O'Nolan were published in R. Christiansen, 'The people of the North', *Lochlann*, 2 (1962), 137–64 at 155–64. The English translation is available online at www.ucc.ie/celt/published/T201041/index.html.

[2] R.B. Warner, 'The Irish souterrains and their background' in H. Crawford

(ed.), *Subterranean Britain: aspects of underground archaeology* (London, 1979), pp 100–44.

3   A. Helgason, C. Lalueza-Fox, S. Ghosh, S. Sigurðardóttir, M.L. Sampietro et al., 'Sequences from first settlers reveal rapid evolution in Icelandic mtDNA pool', *PLoS Genetics*, 5:1 (2009), e1000343 DOI: 10.1371/journal.pgen.1000343.

4   P. Holm, 'The slave trade of Dublin, ninth to twelfth centuries', *Peritia*, 5 (1986), 317–45. A general reference is made to this paper for all information not specifically annotated.

5   *AU*, pp 306–7, *s.a.* 847.

6   N. Skyum-Nielsen, 'Træl', *Kulturhistorisk Leksikon*, 19 (22 vols, Copenhagen, 1956–78), xix.

7   F. O'Toole, 'A history of Ireland in 100 objects' (Dublin, 2013): www.100objects.ie/portfolio-items/39-slave-chain/.

8   'Law of Sjælland, *c.*1200': '*En um swa kan comma at annar takir nokir frelsan man oc rijstir han a andre noos. tha bøde han fare fierthung mannbota. En um han rijstir man at bathum nosum. Tha bøde han fore halwa manbødir. For thy at thz ær threls merke oc ey frels mans*': J. Brøndum-Nielsen, J. Aakjær og Erik Kroman et al. (eds), *Danmarks gamle Landskabslove med Kirkelovene, I–X* (Copenhagen, 1933–61).

9   *The Book of Settlements*, ed. and trans. H. Pálsson and P. Edwards (Winnipeg, MB, 1972), p. 63.

10 F. Amory, 'The historical worth of Rígsþula', *Alvíssmál*, 10 (2001), 3–20.

11 D. Warner (ed.), *Ottonian Germany: the chronicon of Thietmar of Merseburg* (Manchester, 2001); *Adam of Bremen, history of the archbishops of Hamburg-Bremen*, trans. F.J. Tschan (New York, 2002); R.N. Frye (ed.), *Ibn Fadlan's journey to Russia: a tenth-century traveler from Baghdad to the Volga river* (Princeton, NJ, 2005).

12 T. Iversen, *Treldomen. Norsk slaveri i middelalderen* (Bergen, 1997).

13 J.R.C. Hamilton, *Excavations at Jarlshof, Shetland* (Edinburgh, 1956), p. 111.

14 William of Malmesbury, *Gesta regum Anglorum*, ed. R.A.B. Mynors (Oxford, 1998), p. 363.

15 C. Verlinden, *L'esclavage dans l'Europe medievale* (2 vols, Bruges and Ghent, 1955–77).

16 Warner of Rouen, *Moriuht: a Norman Latin poem from the early eleventh century*, ed. and trans. C.J. McDonough (Toronto, 1995).

17 P. Holm, 'Manning and paying the Hiberno-Norse Dublin fleet' in E. Purcell, P. MacCotter, J. Nyhan and J. Sheehan (eds), *Clerics, kings and Vikings: essays on medieval Ireland in honour of Donnchadh Ó Corráin* (Dublin, 2014).

[18] A. Pearson, 'Piracy in late Roman Britain: a perspective from the Viking Age', *Britannia*, 37 (2006), 337–53.

The Mother's Tale

[1] *Med. Ire.*, p. 383.

[2] S. Geraghty, *Viking Dublin: botanical evidence from Fishamble Street* (Dublin, 1996), p. 59.

[3] J.C. Russell, *British medieval population* (Albuquerque, NM, 1948), pp 180–2, tables 8.3–8.6.

[4] For a basic description, see P.F. Wallace, *The Viking Age buildings of Dublin* (2 pts, Dublin, 1992), i, pp 9–14; ii, figs 32–3.

[5] On which the classic work remains F.J. Byrne, *Irish kings and high-kings* (2nd ed. Dublin, 2001).

[6] *NHI*, ix, p. 134.

[7] D. Ó Corráin, 'Women in early Irish society' in M. Mac Curtain and D. Ó Corráin (eds), *Women in Irish society: the historical dimension* (Dublin, 1978), p. 4; F. Kelly, *A guide to early Irish law* (Dublin, 1988), pp 70–1.

[8] Kelly, *Guide to early Irish law*, pp 79, 134.

[9] Ibid., p. 74; Ó Corráin, 'Women in early Irish society', pp 4–6.

[10] Ó Corráin, 'Women in early Irish society', pp 7–8. For a general survey, see S. Shahar, *The fourth estate: a history of women in the Middle Ages*, trans. C. Galai (London and New York, 1983) and, for a wide range of texts, C. McCarthy (ed.), *Love, sex and marriage in the Middle Ages: a sourcebook* (London and New York, 2004).

[11] W.A. Trindade, 'Irish Gormlaith as a sovereignty figure', *Études Celtiques*, 23 (1986), 154–5.

[12] *AU*, pp 414–15, *s.a.* 980; *CS*, pp 226–7, *s.a.* 980; *AFM*, ii, pp 708–13, *s.a.* 980.

[13] M.C. Dobbs, 'The Ban-Shenchus', *Revue Celtique*, 48 (1931), 189.

[14] R.I. Best, O. Bergin, M.A. O'Brien and A. O'Sullivan (eds), *The Book of Leinster, formerly Lebar na Núachongbála* (6 vols, Dublin, 1954–83), iv, p. 1462; M.A. O'Brien (ed.), *Corpus genealogiarum Hiberniae* (Dublin, 1962), p. 13.

[15] *AFM*, ii, pp 820–1, *s.a.* 1030.

[16] For this spirited translation, see D. Ó Cróinín, *Early medieval Ireland, 400–1200* (London and New York, 1995), p. 263. At that time the Rock of Cashel was still a royal stronghold.

[17] *AFM*, ii, pp 820–1, *s.a.* 1030.

[18] *NHI*, ix, p. 131.

19 *AU*, pp 420–1, *s.a.* 989; *CS*, pp 230–1, *s.a.* 989; *AFM*, ii, pp 722–5, *s.a.* 988.

20 Járnkné and Máel Sechnaill were half-brothers: M. Ní Mhaonaigh, *Brian Boru: Ireland's greatest king?* (Stroud, 2007), p. 18.

21 *CS*, pp 232–3, *s.a.* 989.

22 Ní Mhaonaigh, *Brian Boru*, p. 32.

23 *AU*, pp 428–9, *s.a.* 999; *CS*, pp 236–7, *s.a.* 999; *AFM*, ii, pp 738–41, *s.a.* 998; A. MacShamhráin, 'The Battle of Glenn Máma, Dublin, and the high-kingship of Ireland: a millennial commemoration' in S. Duffy (ed.), *Medieval Dublin II* (Dublin, 2001), pp 53–64.

24 J.H. Todd (ed.), *Cogadh Gaedhel re Gallaibh; the war of the Gaedhil with the Gaill* (London, 1867), pp 142–3, 150–3; E.Ó. Sveinsson (ed.), *Brennu-Njáls saga* (Reykjavík, 1954), p. 442; M. Magnusson and H. Pálsson (trans.), *Njal's saga* (London, 1960), p. 342.

25 Ní Mhaonaigh, *Brian Boru*, pp 83–4.

26 D. Ó Corráin, 'Viking Ireland – afterthoughts' in H.B. Clarke, M. Ní Mhaonaigh and R. Ó Floinn (eds), *Ireland and Scandinavia in the early Viking Age* (Dublin, 1998), pp 447–52.

27 Ibid., p. 451.

28 Todd, *Cogadh Gaedhel re Gallaibh*, pp 190–1, where Gormlaith is not mentioned by name.

29 1 Kings 17–19, 21; 2 Kings 9.

30 See, for example, J.L. Nelson, 'Queens as Jezebels: the careers of Brunhild and Balthild in Merovingian history' in D. Baker (ed.), *Medieval women* (Oxford, 1978), pp 31–77; P. Stafford, *Queen Emma and Queen Edith: queenship and women's power in eleventh-century England* (Oxford, 1997).

31 M. Ní Mhaonaigh, 'Tales of three Gormlaiths in medieval Irish literature', *Ériu*, 52 (2002), 24.

32 E.W. Heckett, *Viking Age headcoverings from Dublin* (Dublin, 2003), illustrated at pp 5, 48.

33 M. Dunlevy, *Dress in Ireland* (2nd ed. Cork, 1999), p. 21.

34 Sveinsson, *Brennu-Njáls saga*, p. 440; Magnusson and Pálsson, *Njal's saga*, p. 342.

35 *AT*, p. 371, *s.a.* 1030; *CS*, pp 268–9, *s.a.* 1030; *AI*, pp 196–7, *s.a.* 1030; cf. *AFM*, ii, pp 820–1, *s.a.* 1030.

36 Discussed in S. Kinsella, 'From Hiberno-Norse to Anglo-Norman, *c.*1030–1300' in K. Milne (ed.), *Christ Church Cathedral, Dublin: a history* (Dublin, 2000), pp 28–32; H.B. Clarke, 'Conversion, church and cathedral: the diocese of

Dublin to 1152' in J. Kelly and D. Keogh (eds), *History of the Catholic diocese of Dublin* (Dublin, 2000), pp 33–40.

The Farmer's Tale

[1] For information on farming in early medieval Ireland, see F. Kelly, *Early Irish farming* (Dublin, 1997).

[2] *AFM*, ii, p. 853, *s.a.* 1047.

[3] For information on housing in early medieval Ireland, see A. O'Sullivan et al. (eds), 'Early medieval dwellings and settlements in Ireland, AD400–1100', *Early medieval archaeology project* (EMAP), vol. 1 (2 vols, Dec. 2010): i, available at www.ucd.ie/archaeology/documentstore/allreports/emap–report–4.2vol1–print .pdf.

[4] H. Kenward, A. Hall, E. Allison and J. Carott, 'Environment, activity and living conditions at Deer Park Farms: evidence from plant and invertebrate remains' in C.J. Lynn and J.A. McDowell (eds), *Deer Park Farms: the excavation of a raised rath in the Glenarm valley, Co. Antrim* (Norwich, 2011), pp 498–547.

[5] R. McLaughlin, *Early Irish satire* (Dublin, 2008), p. 155.

[6] A.T. Lucas, 'Footwear in Ireland', *Journal of the County Louth Archaeological Society*, 13:4 (1956), 309–94.

[7] D. O'Rourke, 'First steps in medieval footwear', *Archaeology Ireland*, 5:1 (1991), 22–3.

[8] D. Binchy, 'Bretha Déin Chécht', *Ériu*, 20 (1966), 1–66 at 22–3.

[9] A.O. Anderson and M.O. Anderson, *Adomnán's Life of Columba* (Oxford, 1991), pp 149–51.

[10] K.J. Knudson, B. O'Donnabhain, C. Carver, R. Cleland and T.D. Price, 'Migration and Viking Dublin: paleomobility and paleodiet through isotopic analyses', *Journal of Archaeological Science*, 39:2 (2012), 308–20.

[11] Geraghty, *Viking Dublin*, pp 38–9.

The Tax Collector's Tale

[1] Mt 21: 31–2; Lk 19: 2–9.

[2] *Alen's reg.*, pp 34–5.

[3] Ibid., p. 66.

[4] Ibid., pp 64–5.

[5] *The Irish pipe roll of 14 John, 1211–12*, ed. O. Davies and D.B. Quinn, *Ulster Journal of Archaeology*, 4, supplement (July 1941), 11.

[6] *Alen's reg.*, p. 116.

[7] *CPR*, iv, p. 522.

[8] *Alen's Reg.*, pp 120–3.

[9] NAI, RC 8/1, p. 602.

[10] *CDI*, ii, *1252–84*, p. 244, no. 1313.

[11] *CDI*, ii, *1252–84*, pp 248–9, no. 1341.

[12] Ibid., pp 561–2, no. 2344.

[13] *CDI*, iii, *1285–92*, pp 93–105, no. 215.

[14] *CDI*, iv, *1293–1301*, pp 155–6, no. 332; pp 210–11, no. 443; p. 224, no. 475; p. 240, no. 528; pp 245–6, no. 549; p. 278, no. 586; pp 291–2, no. 612.

[15] *VCH*, iv, Essex, pp 296–302.

[16] *CDI*, iv, *1293–1301*, pp 33–4, no. 48; pp 41–2, no. 90; p. 66, no. 130.

[17] NAI, RC 8/5, pp 308, 323, 337, 339.

[18] *CDI*, iii, *1285–92*, pp 386–9, no. 855.

[19] *CDI*, iv, *1293–1301*, pp 112–17, no. 264.

[20] *CDI*, iii, *1285–92*, pp 46–62, no. 149; pp 118–27, no. 271; pp 185–93, no. 434; *Irish pipe roll of 14 John, 1211–12*, p. 11.

[21] *CDI*, iii, *1285–92*, pp 386–9, no. 855; *CDI*, iv, *1293–1301*, pp 112–17, no. 264.

[22] NAI, RC 8/4, p. 468; RC 8/5, p. 308.

[23] Á. Foley, *The royal manors of medieval Co. Dublin: crown and community* (Dublin, 2013), p. 216.

[24] *CDI*, iii, *1285–92*, pp 430–8, no. 965.

[25] NAI, EX 2/1, p. 174.

[26] Á. Foley, 'The sheriff of Dublin in the fourteenth century' in S. Duffy (ed.), *Medieval Dublin XII* (Dublin, 2012), p. 281.

[27] *CDI*, iii, *1285–92*, pp 298–301, no. 598.

[28] *RDKPRI*, xxxix, p. 38.

[29] *CDI*, iv, *1293–1301*, pp 373–82, no. 825.

[30] *RDKPRI*, xlii, p. 18.

[31] *RDKPRI*, xlv, p. 24; NAI, EX 8/4, p. 999.

The Archdeacon's Tale

[1] Geoffrey Chaucer, *The Canterbury Tales*, N. Coghill (London, 1951), p. 317.

[2] Gerald of Wales, *Gemma ecclesiastica*, ed. J.S. Brewer (2 vols, London, 1862), ii, p. 325.

[3] *CDI*, iii, *1285–92*, p. 297, no. 595.

The Crusader's Tale

[1] K. Hurlock, *Britain, Ireland and the Crusades, c.1100–1300* (Basingstoke, 2013).

[2] J. Riley-Smith, *The Knights Hospitaller in the Levant, c.1070–1309* (Basingstoke

and New York, 2012), pp 15–26; J. Riley-Smith, *Hospitallers: the history of the Order of St John* (London, 1999); H. Nicholson, *The Knights Hospitaller* (Woodbridge, 2001). I am very grateful to Paolo Virtuani for allowing me to use his unpublished research on the Hospitallers and for advice and references relating to various aspects of the order's presence in Ireland.

3. Hurlock, *Britain, Ireland and the crusades*, pp 142–65.

4. J.T. Gilbert (ed.), *Historical and municipal documents of Ireland, 1172–1320, from the archives of the city of Dublin* (Dublin, 1870), pp 495–501.

5. K. Hurlock, *Wales and the crusades 1095–1291* (Cardiff, 2011), pp 133–75.

6. *CDI*, i, *1171–1251*, p. 19, no. 123; J. Delaville Le Roulx (ed.), *Cartulaire général de l'ordre des Hospitaliers de Saint-Jean de Jérusalem (1100–1310)* (4 vols, Paris, 1894–1906), ii, no. 1394.

7. H. Nicholson, 'Serving king and crusade: the military orders in royal service in Ireland, 1220–1400' in N. Housley and M. Bull (eds), *The experience of Crusading* (2 vols, Cambridge, 2003), i, pp 233–55.

8. Ibid., pp 246–8.

9. N. Byrne, *The Irish crusade: a history of the Knights Hospitaller, the Knights Templar and the Knights of Malta in the south-east of Ireland* (Dublin, 2007), pp 177–8.

10. P. Connolly, *Medieval record sources* (Dublin, 2002), pp 14–15.

11. *CDI*, ii, *1252–84*, p. 200, no. 1146.

12. C. Litton Falkiner, 'The Hospital of St John of Jerusalem in Ireland', *PRIA*, 26 (1907), 275–317 at 297.

13. Riley-Smith, *The Knights Hospitaller in the Levant*, p. 185.

14. S. Lloyd, 'The Lord Edward's crusade, 1270–2: its setting and significance' in J. Gillingham and J.C. Holt (eds), *War and government in the Middle Ages: essays in honour of J.O. Prestwich* (Woodbridge, 1984), pp 120–33.

15. Riley-Smith, *The Knights Hospitaller in the Levant*, pp 135, 194.

16. *CDI*, iii, *1285–92*, pp 369–71, no. 814.

17. Nicholson, 'Serving king and crusade', p. 241.

18. Ibid., pp 240, 249.

The Wife's Tale

1. J. Smyly, 'Old deeds in the library of Trinity College', *Hermathena*, 69 (1967), 31–48 at 31–2, no. 69.

2. J. McMurrow, 'Women in medieval Dublin: an introduction' in S. Duffy (ed.), *Medieval Dublin II* (Dublin, 2001), pp 205–15.

The Mason's Tale

[1] Italics and emphasis are the author's own: J. Harvey, *English medieval architects: a biographical dictionary down to 1550* (2nd ed. Gloucester, 1984), pp xii–xiii.

[2] Ibid., p. 82; BL, Egerton MS 1773, fo. 22; *RPH*, p. 116, no. 18.

[3] *RPH*, p. 128, no. 246.

[4] *CARD*, i, pp 26–7; *CIRCLE*, patent roll 9 Richard II, no. 93.

[5] J. Warburton, J. Whitelaw and R. Walsh, *History of the city of Dublin: from the earliest accounts to the present time; containing its annals, antiquities, ecclesiastical history and charters* (2 vols, London, 1818), i, p. 180.

[6] W. Harris (ed.), *The whole works of Sir James Ware concerning Ireland* (Dublin, 1739–64), p. 333.

The Notary's Tale

[1] T. O'Byrne, 'Dublin's Hoccleve: James Yonge, scribe, author and bureaucrat, and the literary world of late medieval Dublin' (PhD, Notre Dame, 2012), pp 437, 462 (trans.).

[2] *Three prose versions of the Secreta secretorum*, ed. R. Steele (London, 1898), p. 212.

[3] Translations are my own. L. Kerns has also produced a modern translation: *The secret of secrets (Secreta secretorum): a modern translation*, ed. L. Kerns (New York, 2008).

[4] *Three prose versions of the Secreta secretorum*, ed. Steele, p. 212.

[5] Ibid.

[6] J.L. Robinson, 'Of the ancient deeds of the parish of St John, Dublin', *PRIA* (1916), 175–224 at 192.

[7] Robinson, 'Of the ancient deeds', 194. For details of Oxmantown, see E. Purcell, 'Land-use in medieval Oxmantown' in S. Duffy (ed.), *Medieval Dublin IV* (Dublin, 2003), pp 193–228.

[8] M. Haren and Y. de Pontfarcy, *Medieval pilgrimage to St Patrick's purgatory and the European tradition* (Enniskillen, 1988), p. 46.

[9] O'Byrne, 'Dublin's Hoccleve', p. 235.

[10] Ibid.

[11] Ibid., pp 460–1.

[12] Ibid., p. 461.

[13] *Three prose versions of the Secreta secretorum*, ed. Steele, p. 121.

[14] Ibid.

[15] Ibid., p. 122.

[16] E. Matthew, 'Foreword', *The secret of secrets*, ed. L. Kerns, xv, vii. See also C.

Whelan, 'James Yonge and the writing of history in late medieval Dublin' in S. Duffy (ed.), *Medieval Dublin XIII* (Dublin, 2013), pp 183–95.

[17] *Three prose versions of the Secreta secretorum*, ed. Steele, p. 129.

[18] For the biblical illusions of this passage, see Whelan, 'James Yonge and the writing of history', p. 189.

[19] R. Frame, 'The defence of the English lordship, 1250–1450' in T. Bartlett and K. Jeffery (eds), *A military history of Ireland* (Cambridge, 1996), pp 76–98 at p. 86.

[20] Steele, *Three prose versions of the Secreta secretorum*, p. 164.

[21] Ibid.

[22] Ibid., p. 160.

[23] *CIRCLE*, patent roll 8 Henry V, no. 22.

The Knight's Tale

[1] W. Fitzgerald, 'Notes on the St Lawrences, lords of Howth, from the end of the twelfth to the middle of the sixteenth century, with a description of the family altar-tomb in St Mary's Church at Howth', *JRSAI*, 5th ser., 37:4 (1907), 353.

[2] *CARD*, i, pp 19–20; N. Brady, 'Dublin's maritime setting and the archaeology of its medieval harbours' in J. Bradley, A.J. Fletcher and A. Simms (eds), *Dublin in the medieval world* (Dublin, 2009), pp 295–315.

[3] F. Elrington Ball, *Howth and its owners: being the fifth part of a history of County Dublin and an extra volume of the Royal Society of Antiquaries of Ireland* (Dublin, 1917), pp 50–1, 58–9.

[4] V. McGowan-Doyle, *The Book of Howth: the Elizabethan re-conquest of Ireland and the Old English* (Cork, 2011), p. 46.

[5] Christopher St Lawrence, 'The Book of Howth' in *CCM*, v, p. 94.

[6] Ibid., p. 87.

[7] McGowan-Doyle, *Book of Howth*, p. 14; *NHI*, ix, p. 506.

[8] Ball, *Howth and its owners*, p. 61.

[9] Ibid., p. 63.

[10] I.D. Aikenhead, 'Students of the common law, 1590–1615: lives and ideas at the inns of court', *University of Toronto Law Journal*, 27:3 (1977), 247.

[11] P. Brand, 'Irish law students and lawyers in late medieval England', *IHS*, 32:126 (2000), 167–9.

[12] J.L. Bolton, 'Irish migration to England in the late Middle Ages: the evidence of 1394 and 1440', *IHS*, 32:125 (2000), 1–21.

[13] C. Lennon, 'St Lawrence, Christopher, seventh Baron Howth (d. 1589)', *Oxford dictionary of national biography* (Oxford, 2004), available at www.oxforddnb.com/view/article/24507, accessed 3 Dec. 2013.

[14] St Lawrence, 'The Book of Howth', p. 201.

[15] Anonymous, 'A treatise for the Reformation of Ireland', *Irish Jurist*, 16 (1981), 308.

[16] S. Ellis, *Ireland in the age of the Tudors, 1447–1603: English expansion and the end of Gaelic rule* (Harlow, 1998), p. 115; T. Clavin and A.M. McCormack, 'Robert Cowley', *DIB* (dib.cambridge.org).

[17] St Lawrence, 'The Book of Howth', pp 192–3.

[18] Edmund Spenser, *A view of the present state of Ireland* on CELT: www.ucc.ie/celt/published/E500000–001/index.html.

[19] St Lawrence, 'The Book of Howth', p. 222.

[20] Ibid., pp 213–14

[21] J. Crawford, *Anglicizing the government of Ireland: the Irish Privy Council and the expansion of Tudor rule, 1556–1578* (Dublin, 1993), pp 240–1.

[22] McGowan-Doyle, *Book of Howth*, p. 29.

[23] Ellis, *Ireland in the age of the Tudors*, p. 184.

The Man of Law's Tale

[1] *CCM*, ii, p. 485.

[2] T. Crowley, *The politics of language in Ireland, 1366–1922: a sourcebook* (London, 2000), p. 28.

[3] Edmund Campion, *Opuscula omnia*, ed. R. Turner (Cologne, 1625) in A.F. Allison and D.M. Rogers (eds), *The contemporary printed literature of the English Counter-Reformation between 1558 amd 1640* (2 vols, Aldershot, 1989–94), i, p. 208, no. 1296.

[4] Richard Stanihurst, 'The description of Ireland' in Holinshed's *Chronicles of England, Scotland and Ireland* (6 vols, London, 1808), vi, p. 34.

[5] Ibid.

[6] *Calendar of state papers relating to Ireland, of the reigns of Henry VIII, Edward VI, Mary and Elizabeth, 1509–1573*, ed. H. Hamilton (London, 1860), p. 454.

The Poet's Tale

[1] O. Bergin, *Irish bardic poetry*, ed. D. Greene and F. Kelly (Dublin, 1970), pp 3–22; E. Knott, *Filíocht na Sgol: Irish classical poetry, commonly called Bardic poetry* (Dublin, 1960).

[2] Bergin, *Irish bardic poetry*, pp 132, 272.

[3] D. Greene, 'The professional poets' in B. Ó Cuív (ed.), *Seven centuries of Irish learning, 1000–1700* (Dublin, 1961), pp 45–57; K. Simms, 'Irish literature: bardic

poetry' in J.R. Strayer (ed.), *Dictionary of the Middle Ages* (13 vols, New York, 1985), vi, pp 53–9.

4 L. Breatnach (ed.), *Uraicecht na Ríar* (Dublin, 1987), p. 46.

5 For information about the Mac Bruaideadha family in Co. Clare, I am much indebted to Luke McInerney, who very kindly allowed me access in advance of publication to his article 'Lettermoylan of Clann Bhruaideadha: a résumé of their landholding, topography and history', *North Munster Archaeological Journal*, 52 (2012), 81–113. See also C. Magrath, 'Materials for a history of Clann Bhruaideadha', *Éigse*, 4:1 (1943), 48–66; D. Ó Murchadha, 'The origins of Clann Bhruaideadha', *Éigse*, 31 (1999), 121–30.

6 L. Miller and E. Power (eds), *Holinshed's Irish chronicle, 1577* (Dublin, 1979), pp 16–17.

7 L. Breatnach, '*Araile felmac féig don Mumain*: unruly pupils and the limitations of satire', *Ériu*, 59 (2009), 111–37.

8 A. Dooley, '*Námha agus cara dár gceird*: A *dán leathaoire*', *Celtica*, 18 (1986), 145–6.

9 S. Mac Airt (ed.), *Leabhar Branach* (Dublin, 1944), pp 215–16.

10 'Mairg riamh ar a raibhe an chos. rug mé san áit ar fhéachos / mo sciath a ttráth a thurbhuidh . a nÁth Cliath 'na cheathrumhnaibh. / Mairg do osguil an abhra. tug orm an ceann cathardha, / an lúdh gan anam d'fhaiscin, nó an chalann úr ordhairc-sin' (ibid., pp 151–3).

11 'Ceathra boill brisde na ruag. do-chonnarc uaim a nÁth Cliath, / dá gcomhroinn ar cheithre spairr. tug mo chroidhe fá dhall chiach' (ibid., pp 153–5).

12 H. Hore, 'Irish bardism, 1561', *Ulster Journal of Archaeology*, 1st ser., 6 (1858), 165–7, 202–12 at 167.

13 Ibid.

14 *AFM*, vi, pp 2320–1, *s.a.* 1602.

15 T. Ó Cléirigh, 'A poem-book of the O Donnells', *Éigse*, 1:1 (1939), 51–61 at 58; L. McKenna (ed.), *Iomarbhágh na bhFileadh: The contention of the bards* (2 vols, London, 1918), ii, pp 204–6; T. Ó Rathile, *Dánta grádha* (Cork, 1925), pp 129–31. See Ó Murchadha, 'The origins of Clann Bhruaideadha', 128.

16 *AFM*, i, pp lxvi–lxvii.

17 *AFM*, vi, p. 2013, *s.a.* 1597.

18 J.W. Stubbs, *The history of the University of Dublin, 1591–1800* (Dublin, 1889), p. 22.

19 Ibid., p. 26.

[20] T. Ó Donnchadha (ed.), *An Leabhar Muimhneach* (Dublin, [1940]), pp 387–98. See *AFM*, vi, pp 2320–1, *s.a.* 1602.

[21] T.F. O'Rahilly (ed.), *Measgra dánta*, i (Cork, 1927), pp 41–4, 79–81.

[22] B. Ó Cuív, 'The earl of Thomond and the poets, AD1572', *Celtica*, 12 (1977), 125–45.

[23] S.H. O'Grady and R. Flower, *Catalogue of Irish manuscripts in the British Museum [al. British Library]* (3 vols, London, 1926, repr. Dublin, 1992), i, p. 394.

[24] L. Mac Cionaith (ed.), *Dioghluim Dána* (Dublin, 1938), no. 95.

[25] *AFM*, vi, pp 2102–5, *s.a.* 1599.

[26] Magrath, 'Materials', p. 61, n. 17; B. Ó Cuív, 'The Irish language in the early modern period' in *NHI*, iii, pp 509–45 at pp 511–12.

[27] P. Walsh, *The Four Masters and their work* (Dublin, 1944), pp 25–31.

[28] D. Ó Riain-Raedel, 'The travels of Irish manuscripts: from the Continent to Ireland' in T. Barnard, D. Ó Cróinín and K. Simms (eds), *A miracle of learning* (Aldershot, 1998), pp 52–67 at pp 53–4.

[29] Ó Cuív, 'The Irish language', pp 522, 530, 532.

[30] McKenna, *Iomarbhágh*, i, pp 148–75, verses 8–11, 17–19, 38–9, 107–14, 173–6.

[31] Mac Cionaith, *Dioghluim dána*, nos 2, 17, 51; D. McManus and E. Ó Raghallaigh (eds), *A bardic miscellany* (Dublin, 2010), no. 34.

[32] B. Ó Cuív, *Catalogue of Irish language manuscripts in the Bodleian Library at Oxford and Oxford College Libraries* (2 vols, Dublin, 2001).

Glossary

❦

Arris	A sharp angle where two facets meet.
Boulder clay	Undisturbed natural clay.
Canon	A clergyman living with others in a clergy-house, or in one of the houses within the precinct or close of a cathedral or collegiate church, and ordering his life according to the canons or rules of the church (OED).
Carucate	A measure of land, which varied based on the nature of the soil etc. and amounted to as much as could be tilled with one plough in a year (OED).
Chancery	The secretariat of the Dublin government, which issued letters bearing the Irish great seal in the name of the king. Some of these letters included writs of summons to parliament and copies of English statutes for circulation in Ireland (*Med. Ire.*).
Currency	*l.* was the symbol for a pound in medieval (Latin) sources, from the Latin *libra* (plural *librae*). Shillings were indicated by an *s.* for *solidus* (plural *solidi*), while pence were indicated by a *d.* for *denarius* (plural *denarii*). There are 12 pence in a shilling and 20 shillings in a pound.
Cutwaters	The wedge-shaped up-river and down-river sides of a bridge pier, designed to divide the current. These are sometimes carried up onto the bridge deck giving the parapet V-shaped pedestrian refuges at road level.
Engrosser	A clerk or copyist responsible for keeping the official records of the exchequer on the great pipe roll.
Exchequer	The chief financial institution in medieval Ireland, headed by the treasurer.

Farthing	A quarter of a penny or the coin representing this value.
Grave-field	A term coined for a group of burials that might be distributed over a large distance, whereas a cemetery is a concentrated, defined (often enclosed) burial place.
Hold the farm	To occupy land for a fixed annual monetary rent.
Issues	Monetary profits. In many cases this refers specifically to profits coming from an ecclesiastical office or holding.
Mark	A unit of medieval financial account equated with two-thirds of a pound sterling or 13 shillings and 4 pence.
Messuage	A portion of land occupied or intended to be occupied, as the site for a dwelling house; (also) a dwelling house together with outbuildings and the adjacent land assigned to its use (OED).
Palisade	A timber fence.
Prebend	The portion of a cathedral church's income assigned for the support of an individual officer or canon. The term also refers to the source of the income, usually a parish church.
Prior	A monastic officer in charge of a priory.
Souterrrain	A narrow underground cellar or gallery.
Strap end	A metal sheath on the end of a belt.
Whittle-tanged knife	A type of knife in which the tang (the part of the knife that extends into the handle) is whittled to a tapered point for insertion into the handle.
Wild Geese	Irish soldiers active on the Continent, particularly those that departed Ireland after the Treaty of Limerick in 1691.

Index